Klett Lektürehilfen

Ray Bradbury

Fahrenheit 451

Interpretationshilfe für Oberstufe und Abitur

von
Peter Bruck

Inhaltsangabe der Lektüre als MP3-Download
unter www.klett-lerntraining.de
Klicken Sie bei Downloads Lektürehilfen an.

Sie können auch direkt auf die Seite gehen mit:
www.klett-lerntraining.de/main/book-03_09-downloads

Klett Lerntraining

Dr. Peter Bruck, apl. Professor für Neuere Amerikanische Literatur an der Universität Osnabrück, Studiendirektor i. R. und ehemaliger Fachbereichsleiter Sprachen am Städtischen Gymnasium Selm.

Die Seitenangaben zum Roman beziehen sich auf die Ausgabe:
Ray Bradbury: Fahrenheit 451. London: HarperVoyager, 2008.

Bibliografische Information der Deutschen Nationalbibliothek
Die Deutsche Nationalbibliothek verzeichnet diese Publikation in der Deutschen Nationalbibliografie; detaillierte bibliografische Daten sind im Internet über http://dnb.dnb.de abrufbar

1. Auflage 2019

www.klett-lerntraining.de
Umschlagfoto: ullstein bild (Roger-Viollet/Jean-Pierre Couderc), Berlin
Satz: DOPPELPUNKT, Stuttgart
Druck: medienhaus Plump GmbH, Rheinbreitbach
Printed in Germany
ISBN 978-3-12-923156-2

The Political and Cultural Background of the Novel

Fahrenheit 451, which is Bradbury's fifth book and his first true novel, deals with four aspects that were topical in the early 1950s. To begin with, the idea of censorship which is central to such short stories as "The Exiles" (1949) and "Usher II" (1950) has been taken up by the author in this novel. Keeping in mind that the novel was conceived when Senator Joseph McCarthy had started his public campaign against communism in general and alleged communist activities in US government institutions in particular it will come as no surprise that the book draws upon the climate of paranoia, irrationality and fear that was prevalent in intellectual circles in the 1950s. The anti-intellectualism of that time is widely reflected in the firemen of *Fahrenheit 451* and their leading figure Captain Beatty.

As the Senate hearings of Joseph McCarthy began to focus on writers and film makers, the question of artistic freedom troubled many people and became the subject of lively debates. It must be pointed out in this context that censorship was at times allowed and even enforced by the United States government. In the early years of film-making, for example, censorship was allowed on the grounds that movies were entertainment and not an expression of free speech. The McCarthy hearings into the political background of artists led to the "blackballing" of several prominent Hollywood writers during the 1950s. While the Supreme Court decision allowing censorship of films was overturned in 1952, strict regulation of film contents persisted in the 1960s. Afterwards attempts to censor artistic products came mainly from organized pressure groups and usually referred to literary texts used in the classroom. An excellent fictional example of this is Nat Hentoff's novel *The Day They Came To Arrest The Book* (1982) which depicts efforts to ban Mark Twain's *Huckleberry Finn* in the classroom. Ironically, Bradbury himself became the victim of such attempts as, unknown to him, a high-school edition of *Fahrenheit 451* was bowdlerized, which means that words viewed as indecent were either deleted or replaced. A good example of this are the following phrases and their deletion or replacement:

> "I saw the damnedest snake in the world the other night [ ]"
> "Jesus God," said Montag. "Every hour so many damn things in the sky! How in hell did those bombers get up there every single second of our lives!" (p. 95 f.)

> "I saw the craziest snake in the world the other night."
> "Every hour so many things in the sky!" said Montag. "How did those bombers get up there every single second of our lives!" (Eller/Touponce, *Ray Bradbury. The Life of Fiction*, pp. 64 f.)

Secondly, another theme of the Cold War years that Bradbury has taken up is the precariousness of human existence in the atomic age. The Soviet Union's acquisition of atomic weapons technology by 1949 and the concomitant end of the US monopoly on thermonuclear weapons raised fears of a nuclear war and a potential annihilation of mankind. The general sense of anxiety as a manifestation of the Cold War is explored in the novels *The Martian Chronicles* and *Fahrenheit 451*. Throughout *Fahrenheit 451* there are numerous references to ongoing wars. Strangely, people view the war as a form of entertainment that has no direct reference to them and much less influence on their lives. Hence the third aspect dealt with is the beginning of mass or consumer culture in the early 1950s which, as Bradbury saw it, is completely divorced from political awareness. The agent of mass culture are the mass media, in particular television, which exclusively shape the people's world view and outlook on life. The novel thus extrapolates certain elements of the American culture of that time.

Bradbury's criticism of mass culture was a visionary draft that was later confirmed by sociological studies. The ideas advanced by Montag and his superior Captain Beatty anticipate certain arguments that were voiced by cultural critics decades later.

The fourth aspect that Bradbury deals with in his novel is the development of robots. With the Mechanical Hound he presents a robot that is more powerful than a human being in its ability to "sniff out" its prey. This representation reflects a then commonly held view that the nature of robots is to be feared because they do not possess human qualities and might even be able to take control over human beings. Many writers and film makers capitalized on this fear by portraying monstrous creatures created by misused technology as well as technology itself turning against its creators. This fear of technology was aptly captured by Bradbury in *Fahrenheit 451*.

2 Analysis and Interpretation

The Story

Part One: The Hearth and the Salamander

Set in an unspecified future the novel opens with Guy Montag, the protagonist, who is introduced at his work. Montag is a fireman, and unlike firemen in our time he does not extinguish fires but rather burns books that are illegal in the futuristic society depicted by the novel. Burning books gives him "a special pleasure" (p. 9), the narrator even compares his hands holding the igniter to "the hands of some amazing conductor playing all the symphonies of blazing and burning" (ibid.).

The opening paragraph introduces a major literary device that is central to the understanding of the way the author handles the depiction of this future world. By having the firemen lighting fires instead of putting them out Bradbury has reversed their traditional role. Hence he makes use of the technique of reversal (see Outline 6 on p. 73 of this study aid).

As Montag walks home from his work he meets Clarisse McClellan, his 17-year-old new neighbour. The colour of her dress and her "milk-white" (p. 12) complexion contrast sharply with Montag's black fireman uniform which displays a "salamander on his arm and [a] phoenix-disc on his chest" (ibid.). The contrast of colours and the emblems on Montag's uniform show two additional literary devices that are put to use from the very beginning. Bradbury uses antithetical contrasts and colour symbolism to characterize his figures and the atmosphere of their surroundings. What is more, he employs a complex set of animal imagery that is associated with the firemen and, in particular, with Montag. Whereas the title of this section "The Hearth and the Salamander" alludes to images of fire and thus of destruction, as the hearth is where the fire is built and burns strongest, the salamander is a lizard which is said to survive in flames. Hence Montag may be seen from the very outset as the person who even when surrounded by flames cannot be crushed by them.

Montag is at once taken aback and at the same time drawn to Clarisse's inquisitiveness and her apparent non-conformity. She loves nature, doesn't watch television and dislikes driving cars all of which are, as it turns out, deviant attitudes in this future society. Significantly, Clarisse questions Montag steadily about his job, his perception of the world and tells him that she comes from a strange family that does such peculiar things as talk to each other and walk (being a pedestrian, like reading, is against the law). She leaves him with the query "Are you happy?" (p. 17), which greatly baffles him. Clarisse's strangeness makes him nervous, and he laughs repeatedly and involuntarily. She reminds him in different ways of candlelight, a clock, and a mirror. Clarisse leaves a strong impression on him and he continues to reflect on their brief encounter and her way of viewing the world which differs so much from his own.

Upon entering his house and walking into his wife's dark bedroom Montag begins to realize that he is "not happy". Repeating these words twice he is struck by a sudden insight: "He recognized this as the true state of affairs" (p. 20) and realizes that his happiness up to this point has been a pretense. The encounter with Clarisse, then, has set in motion the need to review his mental state and his life as a fireman.

When opening the bedroom door Montag has the sensation of walking into a "mausoleum", a "tomb-world" (p. 19). The imagery not only conveys his sense of foreboding but also symbolically underlines the spiritual death of his wife. Inside the bedroom Montag finds his wife Mildred in bed listening to earplug radios called "Seashells," just as he has found her every night for the past two years. By her bed, he accidentally kicks an empty bottle of sleeping pills and calls the hospital when a sonic boom from a squadron of jet bombers shakes the house. Two cynical hospital workers arrive with a machine that pumps Mildred's stomach (Montag later refers to the device as the "Snake") and another one that replaces all her poisoned blood with fresh blood. Neither of the paramedics are medical doctors, a fact that Montag finds odd. However, as the paramedics explain that they perform these kinds of procedures many times a night, this clearly shows another example of the technique of reversal: suicide attempts are seen as regular occurrences in this society, they are not frowned upon or considered pathological. When the paramedics depart, Montag begins to reflect on the impersonal and joyless nature of their marital life which is sharply contrasted with the "[l]aughter [blowing] across the moon-coloured lawn from the house of Clarisse" (p. 26).

The next morning Mildred goes about her daily chores, not recalling the previous night's incident. When Montag tries to discuss it with her, she reacts with complete disbelief, eager to turn her attention to the diversions of the little "Seashells" constantly inserted in her ears and the people on the three-wall television, whom she calls her "family" (p. 65). Their monosyllabic dialogue makes it clear that the communication between husband and wife is devoid of any intimacy and depth.

On his way to work Montag runs into Clarisse again, and again she questions him incessantly about his relationship to his wife and his work, pointing out that to her he is "not like the others", that his being "a fireman [...] just doesn't seem right" (p. 34). The encounter leaves Montag deeply disturbed:

"He felt his body divide itself into a hotness and a coldness [...] the two halves grinding one upon the other." (pp. 34 f) Upon entering the fire station, Montag passes the Mechanical Hound, a robotic police dog, which, once it has been geared to an individual's chemical balance, is able to locate and kill that person. Significantly, the dog growls at him which unsettles Montag. The dog's growling may be seen as foreshadowing Montag's transformation as the Mechanical Hound obviously notices that he has become imbalanced. When Montag speaks about the dog's reaction to his superior Captain Beatty, Beatty dismisses the matter by making patronizing references to both the Hound and Montag's aversion to it.

Throughout the following days Montag sees Clarisse every day and finds himself looking forward to his conversations with the girl whose intense liveliness wakes him up to the fact of real sensations. He is disappointed when he doesn't meet her any more on the corner of the subway but is unable to find out anything about her whereabouts. There are rumours of a possible impending war on the radio and Montag becomes increasingly introspective about his job and the people whose books and homes he destroys. During a card game with his colleagues and Captain Beatty at the fire station he starts wondering if their job had always been like it is now for him: "Didn't firemen *prevent* fires rather than stoke them up and get them going?" (p. 47) When Stoneman and Black confront him with the official history of the Firemen of America it becomes clear that history has been re-written: "Established, 1790, to burn English-influenced books in the Colonies. First Fireman: Benjamin Franklin." (p. 48) The scene at the fire station shows that Montag begins to feel alienated from the other firemen. He realizes suddenly that all of them look exactly like him, with their uniforms, physiques, and grafted-on smiles. This is a physical manifestation of the fact that the dystopian society demands that everyone think and act the same. Montag used to bet with the other firemen on games of releasing animals for the Hound to catch and kill, but now he just lies in his bunk upstairs and listens. He begins to question things no other fireman would ever think of, such as why alarms always come in at night, and whether this is simply because fire is prettier then.

The confrontation between Montag and his colleagues is interrupted by an alarm which calls the firemen to an old house. When they arrive there the woman is still in the house and seems to be in a state of shock, but understands fully why they have come. They show her the complaint "Have reason to suspect attic; 11 no Elm, City. E.B." (p. 49). She recognizes the initials of her neighbour who is the obvious informant. Neither Montag nor the others in his squad have ever had to do their job with the book-owner still present. So they are all flustered by the old woman's presence, but Montag, in particular, seems to feel guilty because of their intrusion into her house and the destruction of her home. While the house is being raided he discreetly picks up a book and hides it under his jacket. As they all run out of the kerosene-drenched house, the elderly lady refuses to leave, even as it becomes difficult for her to breathe in the fumes. Montag pleads with the captain that they must make an effort to remove the woman from the house. He is told to abandon the house quickly and without further question, and the old woman also urges him to leave her, because she obviously is determined to be burned together with her books. As the firemen stand on her front lawn, she shows them the kitchen match she has concealed in her palm. The other firemen quickly back away into the street when seeing this. Montag, however, makes one last attempt to convince the woman to leave, but she refuses, and Beatty does not force her to abandon the house. Montag finally runs out of the house at the very last moment. He turns to watch the old woman lighting the match. She drops the match into the glistening trail of kerosene on her front porch, and is soon engulfed by the burst of flames. Confused and troubled, the firemen silently head back to their station. All of them, except Beatty, who remains cool, are dazed by what has just happened.

The incident instigates Montag's growing alienation from his job. While snatching the book, Montag was able to read one of its lines which is enough to convince him that there must be something in books that, once experienced, makes living life without them meaningless. He realizes that there is a person, an author behind every book. He returns home shaken by the woman's death and nervous about his own illegal deed: "His hands had been infected, and soon it would be his arms. He could feel the poison working up his wrists and into his elbows and his shoulders, and then the jump-over from shoulder-blade to shoulder-blade like a spark leaping a gap. His hands were ravenous." (pp. 55 f) Images of spreading illness suggest that Montag is no longer his conscious, rational self. What is more, the personification of his hands indicates that at this stage Montag lacks awareness of his true motivation and is overpowered by some sort of frenzy. However, his act of defiance, his violation of the rules of his profession is described as a kind of infection rather than a conscious choice.

When Montag and his wife lie in their bed, he finds himself unable to recall how and where they met. He asks Millie if she remembers but she doesn't and is not bothered by it. Montag is overcome with thoughts of his loveless, liveless marriage and recalls the mindless activities that characterize his wife's daily life. For example, she likes driving her car down the highways at tremendous rates of speed, hoping to kill an animal or, better yet, a human being. It becomes clear to him that her life is marked by nothing but various forms of artificial intoxication that are provided by modern technologies. When Montag questions her about Clarisse whom he hasn't seen for days, Mildred says that she had forgotten to tell him that Clarisse was run over by a car and killed four days earlier. Her family then moved out. Montag is extremely upset by these news and is angry with his wife for having forgotten to tell him.

Before he falls asleep with the stolen book under his pillow he believes to hear the Hound outside their house. The actual or virtual presence of the Hound (it remains unclear if it is really there) encapsulates Montag's state of mind: his fear, guilt and his growing sense of emptiness and alienation.
The following morning Montag wakes up feeling ill and unable to go to work. He tells Mildred about burning the old woman and asks her if she would mind if he gave up his job for a while. He tries to make her understand his feelings of guilt at burning the woman and at burning the books, which represent so many people's lives and work, but she will not listen and responds, instead, with disbelief and annoyance rather than compassion. Montag in turn is irritated by her lack of interest in his well-being. Captain Beatty arrives to ask him when he will be well again. He gives Montag what he hopes will be an antidote for his sickness, which consists of a lesson in firemen history. His visit is significant in three respects. First of all, the meeting establishes their respective roles, with Beatty being the teacher and Montag his disciple. Secondly, Beatty's account serves as a didactic lecture by the representative of the system addressed to the reader as well as to Montag. This lecture explains the origins of the system, its ideology and social philosophy. Thirdly, it turns out to be an incisive indictment of the American culture industry of the early 1950s and Bradbury's extrapolation of it.
Thus Beatty lectures Montag on how society has evolved into the current technological age, leaving no room for those who, like Clarisse, deviate from its rigid conformity. Beatty idolizes fire, the power of the state to reduce everything to ashy sameness and death. No minority differences are to be tolerated. Fire to him is an antibiotic for it effectively destroys differences that would inevitably arise from reading books. As an advocate of mass culture, Beatty believes that everyone must be the same and desire the same things. He asserts that people are not born equal but made equal through laws and regulations: "We must all be alike. Not everyone born free and equal [...], but everyone *made* equal. Each man the image of every other; then all are happy, for there are no mountains to make them cower, to judge themselves against." (p. 77) According to him, repetition of the same will produce the greatest happiness for the greatest number of people. Beatty clearly argues here in favour of a conformist, egalitarian society that has done away with individual differences and merits. What he seems to fear most, is a society open to conflicts of thought and interpretation. He clearly wants people to be crammed full of facts that do not change and forego any conflicting views.
In his lecture Beatty paints an increasingly negative picture of history, arguing that modern science and, in particular, philosophy have only managed to uncover a bleak and useless existence that has made mankind feel only bestial and lonely. His evaluation of books clearly marks him as a nihilist: "Well, Montag, take my word for it [...] the books say *nothing*. Nothing you can teach or believe. They're about non-existent people, figments of imagination, if

they're fiction. And if they're non-fiction, it's worse, one professor calling another an idiot, one philosopher screaming down another's gullet." (p. 81) While Beatty is visiting the Montags, Millie nervously seeks to tidy up the bedroom. She tries to fluff Montag's pillow, but because he has hidden a book underneath it he angrily tells her to stop bothering him. Yet Millie does feel the shape of the book and is shocked but does not turn her husband in. Upon leaving the Captain mentions in passing that firemen are occasionally overcome by curiosity about the books they burn and may steal some to satisfy their curiosity. In such a case the fireman is given a 24-hour period to return the book. Otherwise, as Beatty puts it, "we simply come and burn it for him" (p. 82).

Beatty's lecture leaves Montag deeply troubled. It begins to dawn on him that he is not happy, that being a fireman is something to be detested: "I suddenly realized that I didn't like [the firemen] at all, and I didn't like myself at all any more. And I thought maybe it would be best if the firemen themselves were burnt." (p. 87) Quite obviously, Montag has reached a new state of self-awareness which makes him begin to realize the hollowness of his life. He nervously walks about the house and confesses to Mildred that he has secretly put aside some books. When he shows her his collection that he has hidden behind the grille of the air-conditioner Mildred panics, insisting that they burn the books in the incinerator. Before the matter is resolved, someone is at their front door, softly calling for Mrs Montag. Both are terrified and don't answer the door. Eventually the visitor goes away, leaving the Montags alone with their illegal possession of books.

Part One ends with Montag sitting on the kitchen floor together with his wife. He opens a book, and with great anticipation begins to read. He reads many pages aloud until he comes to this passage: "It is computed that eleven thousand persons have at several times suffered death rather than submit to break eggs at the smaller end." (p. 89) Mildred is bewildered: "What does it mean? It doesn't mean *anything*! The Captain was right." (ibid.) Montag has been reading from Swift's satire *Gulliver's Travels*, which contains philosophical reflections on the human condition. Significantly, Mildred cannot even open her mind enough to listen to the words, much less register their meaning. Montag, on the other hand, knows there is meaning in these words and understands that it is his un-read, un-learned mind rather than the book itself that is making it difficult to understand. So he continues, hoping he will eventually grasp the importance of the written words.

The first part of the novel thus introduces the major literary devices (technique of reversal, antithetical contrast, colour symbolism and animal imagery) as well as the setting and some of the major characters. The protagonist Guy Montag is undergoing a change of attitude towards his job and his married life, and he is about to become a dissident as he has illegally stored some books. Furthermore, the society depicted here is not the result of a dictator having seized power but rather, as Captain Beatty puts it, it evolved gradually: "There was no dictum, no declaration, no censorship, to start with, no! Technology, mass exploitation, and minority pressure carried the trick." (p. 65) Hence the suspense created in the first part centres around the question if and how Montag will start to fight the system and whether he will find others who like him have become dissatisfied with the stereotypical happiness decreed by the government.

Part Two: The Sieve and the Sand

Montag spends the afternoon uneasily reading while his wife Mildred is sitting idly in the hall, but he does not really understand what he is reading. The Mechanical Hound comes and sniffs at the door, then leaves without causing a disturbance. When reading Montag is often reminded of Clarisse, he wonders what it was that made her so different from anybody else he knows. Mildred strongly dislikes her husband's reading, whining that their house will be burnt down if anyone finds out. Montag responds with a lecture on their ignorance. He points out that they have no idea about what is going on in the world, he speaks of the ongoing wars and how people all over the world live in misery and poverty while they live well and are able to enjoy their leisure. Montag is interrupted by the ringing of the phone. Mildred answers it and is immediately engaged in a conversation about the television programme. Montag realizes he will never get his wife to help him in his quest. He decides to hide most of the books in the shrubbery in their backyard for fear that Mildred will burn them. While she continues her conversation on the phone, he searches his mind for someone who could be a kind of teacher in his thirst for knowledge.

Montag recalls an encounter with an old Professor of English named Faber that took place about a year ago in a park. It was apparent that Faber had been reading a book of poetry before Montag arrived and that he had hidden the book in his coat. The fireman Montag did nothing about this, he reassured Faber that he was safe. They talked for a while, and Faber gave him his address and telephone number. Montag even remembers some of Faber's words like the following: "I don't talk *things*, sir, I talk the *meaning* of things." (p. 83) He decides to call the old professor who is shocked to hear from him, believing the call to be a trap, as Montag questions him about how many copies of the Bible and Plato and Shakespeare are left in the country. Faber tells him that there are no copies left and hangs up.

Montag goes back to his books and realizes that he has taken from the old woman what may well be the last copy of the Bible in existence. Pondering which of his books to hand over to Beatty Montag wonders if the Captain might know of a specific title he possesses. He decides to have a duplicate made before that night. Meanwhile Mildred tells him that some of her friends are coming over to watch TV with her. He questions his wife about her beloved television characters: "Does your 'family' love you, love you *very* much, love you with all their heart and soul, Millie?" (p. 100) She dismisses the question as "silly", while he is sad and sighs which indicates that he believes his wife to be out of touch with reality, to be living in an artifical world. Montag leaves the house and takes the subway to Faber's apartment. On the way he realizes how "numb" (p. 101) he has become and wonders if he will ever regain his sense of purpose. During the subway ride he recalls an incident from his childhood when he tried to fill a sieve with sand on the beach to get a dime from a mischievous cousin. He compares this recollection to his attempt to read and memorize the whole Bible as quickly as possible in the hope that, if he reads fast enough, some of the material will stay in his mind. He becomes increasingly frustrated as he is continuously distracted by a jingle for a toothpaste. He finally gets up in front of all the passengers and screams at the loudspeaker to shut up, waving his book around. The astonished passengers are about to call a guard, but Montag gets off at the next station. His behaviour at this point suggests that he is in a state of inner turmoil, that he is on the verge of losing control over himself as he has just committed an open act of rebellion in public.

Montag goes to Faber and shows him his book. The old man is nervous at first, but allows Montag in after having made sure that he is alone. He asks the old professor to teach him to understand what he reads. Skipping through Montag's Bible Faber muses about the portrayal of Christ on television, saying that "Christ is one of the 'family' now. [...] He's a regular peppermint stick now, all sugar-crystal and saccharine when he isn't making veiled references to certain commercial products that every worshipper *absolutely* needs" (p. 106). He admits that he was a coward for not having stood up in protest back when the banning of books started. Faber explains to Montag that his not knowing the real reason of his unhappiness is not the disappearance of books as such; what Montag is looking for in reality is the meaning the books contain. The same meaning could be included in media like television or radio, but people no longer demand it. Faber asserts that books are feared because "[t]hey show the pores in the face of life" (p. 108), because they make people uncomfortable by making them think. He goes on to note that the world needs the kind of quality of information that used to be found in books, the leisure to analyze and understand that information and the right to act on that understanding.

Montag develops a plan to bring down the oppressive system by planting books in the homes of firemen to discredit their profession and see their houses burn. Faber doesn't believe, however, that this action would get to the heart of the matter, saying that people are having too much fun to care about the issue. He points out that firemen are not really necessary to ban books because the public stopped reading them of its own will even before they were burned. He suggests, instead, they should wait for the impending war to implode society so that they could start anew. Quite obviously the old professor is completely disheartened by the state of affairs and feels utterly helpless to do anything to bring about a change. Montag begins tearing pages from the Bible in order to make Faber help him. He succeeds as the old man finally agrees to ask an old and trusted friend of his to print copies of books for them. Montag worries that he will not be able to cope with Captain Beatty's persuasive rhetoric that night. Hence Faber gives him a small two-way radio that he has invented himself and that is similar in shape to the seashell radio used by Mildred. They plan to communicate via the radio; Faber will listen to everything Montag says and provide rhetorical assistance. Montag leaves the professor's apartment and goes to an all-night bank to withdraw money from his bank account which he will later give to Faber so that he can pay his friend to print the books. Outside he listens to reports on the radio which contain the following information: "We have mobilized a million men. Quick victory is ours if the war comes" (p. 119). Faber and Montag talk to each other via the radio, with Montag wondering "when do I start working things out on my own" and Faber responding "You've started already. By saying what you just said" (p. 120). Montag returns home and is eating in the kitchen when his wife's friends, Mrs Phelps and Mrs Bowles, arrive to watch television with Mildred. The ladies promptly disappear into the TV parlour. Montag, who is greatly disturbed by the women's mindless chatter, becomes so enraged that he unplugs the television walls and tries to engage the women in a discussion about the impending war. Mrs Phelps is totally disinterested as is shown by her lack of concern for her third husband who has gone off to fight; she quickly turns the conversation back to television programmes. Montag is persisting, however, questioning the women about their children. As it turns out, Mrs Phelps has none and Mrs Bowles has two for whom she obviously feels no love. The conversation briefly turns to politics, and Montag is disgusted to learn that the women voted for the current president for the sole reason that he was more handsome than his rival candidate. He then takes out a book of poetry and shows it to the shocked ladies. Mildred invents a quick lie, explaining that every fireman is allowed to bring home one book a year to see how silly they are. Faber tells Montag via the radio to agree to this. Mildred urges him to read something "funny", and Montag begins to read aloud from the last two stanzas of Matthew Arnold's "Dover Beach", one of the most famous poems in the English language. The effect of this reading on Mildred and her friends who are accustomed only to TV series like "that Dove five-minute romance" on the wall-sized screens is stunning. One woman sobs uncontrollably, the other becomes enraged at being exposed to so much "poetry and sickness": "Silly words, silly words, silly awful hurting words" (p. 131). Montag himself is overcome by the sudden appearance of authentic feelings and deep communication in the midst of "an empty desert" (p. 129), which is what the living-room is compared to after the television screens have been switched off and the idle chatter has stopped. Mildred tries to calm her agitated friends, but the women are so shaken that they leave. Upon their leaving Montag shouts at the women to think about the emptiness in their lives. Mildred disappears into the bathroom to take some sleeping pills and Montag removes the radio from his ear as Faber begs him to stop his destructive utterances.

Before Montag leaves for work he discovers that Mildred has obviously started to burn some of the books in the incinerator. He hides the remaining books in the backyard and heads off to the fire station. He puts the radio back into his ear and resumes contact with Faber who advises him to act normally and stay relaxed when he has returned to the fire station. Montag is nervous when he arrives there, he notices that the Mechanical Hound is gone. Wordlessly he hands over his book to Beatty, who throws it into the trashcan without bothering to look at the title. The Captain welcomes him back with the words: "Here comes a very strange beast which in all tongues is called a fool." (p. 136) Montag sits down to play cards with the Captain and the other men. During the card game Beatty seeks to provoke Montag by constantly quoting from literature. Montag becomes so afraid of making a mistake that he cannot move his feet. Meanwhile, Faber advises him all the time to keep quiet, which he does with some difficulty. An alarm comes through, and Beatty glances at the address and takes the wheel of the fire engine. When they arrive at their destination Montag realizes that they have been called to his own home.

The second part of the novel thus ends with a dramatic climax. It focusses on Montag's increasing disillusionment and disdain for all of society where maintaining one's own illusion of happiness is the only priority. Furthermore, the protagonist's growing sense of rebelliousness is shown, his open defiance of society's norms. He is desperately in need of an ally who will stand by his side and act as an intellectual mentor. This role has been taken up by Faber who becomes a kind of opponent to Captain Beatty as the spokesman of the system. The suspense created at the end of the second part, then, centres around the question how Montag will deal with the impending discovery of the books he illegally has put aside, what sort of punishment will await him, how he might manage to get away from Beatty and the others and what sort of future he will have in this oppressive society.

Part Three: Burning Bright

The title of the third part is an allusion to William Blake's famous poem "The Tiger" ("Tiger! Tiger! Burning bright / In the forests of the night, / What immortal hand or eye / Could frame thy fearful symmetry?") and thus refers to the ambiguity of fire as the novel's central symbol.

Upon arriving at his house Montag is initially in a state of utter disbelief. While his fellow firemen are rushing into the house, Mildred who has obviously reported him to the firemen for possessing books comes out and hurries away without a word, suitcase in hand, as the taxi pulls up beside her. Montag calls to her asking if it was her who called the alarm, but she does not pay attention to him. She has absolutely no empathy for her husband and only seems concerned about her TV walls. She mumbles to herself as she sits in the car about her poor family being gone now, and not even once looks at her husband as the taxi speeds away.
Stoneman and Black, the two other firemen on the scene, begin breaking windows in Montag's house for cross-ventilation. Beatty at his side criticizes Montag for his foolishness in believing he could conceal his having books and asks why he hadn't turned them in when the Hound was sniffing around his front door. As Beatty continues to talk to Montag Faber speaks to him via the secret radio, asking him what is going on and telling him to get away. However, Montag tells him that he is trapped, as the Mechanical Hound is nearby and will certainly be after him. Beatty switches on the igniter of a flame-thrower and lectures Montag on the beauty of fire: "What is fire? […] Its real beauty is that it destroys responsibility and consequences. A problem gets too burdensome, then into the furnace with it. Now, Montag, you're a burden. And fire will lift you off my shoulders" (pp. 149 f). With these words Beatty orders him to to burn down his own house, room by room. Montag does what he is ordered to do and destroys all his possessions, beginning with the twin beds, followed by the bedroom walls and Mildred's cosmetic chest. On his way into the parlour to burn the TV walls Beatty shouts at him to burn the books, which Montag does before turning his rage upon the three, now blank walls, which alienated him from his wife. When finished, he stands in front of Beatty, feeling dejected and numb, but still holding on to the flame-thrower. Beatty asks him why he kept the books, but Montag doesn't answer. Beatty sees that Montag is listening to something and strikes him on the head, thereby knocking the secret radio from his ear. Beatty picks it up, saying that he will find out who is at the other end. After the Captain provokes him with literary quotations, his last a quote from Shakespeare's *Julius Caesar*, Montag turns the flame-thrower on him and kills him. The other firemen do not move, and he manages to knock them out. The Mechanical Hound appears and injects an anaesthetic into Montag's leg before he is able to destroy it with his flame-thrower. Montag stumbles away in spite of his numb leg. Before he leaves the ruins of his house he goes into his garden and secures four books which his wife had obviously missed. He hears sirens approaching and tries to continue down an alley but he falls down and begins to cry uncontrollably. It dawns on him that Beatty had wanted to die, that he had known that Montag was going to kill him. His thoughts are interrupted by the sound of footsteps approaching. He forces

himself up and runs until the numbness leaves his leg. He puts a regular seashell into his ear and hears police news about his flight and a warning to people who are ordered to be on the lookout for him.
Montag finds a petrol station and washes the soot from his face to look less suspicious. He hears on the radio that war has been declared. Starting to cross a street he is nearly hit by a car. First he thinks that it is the police coming after him, then he realizes the car's passengers are children who would have killed him for fun. He creeps into one of his fellow firemen's houses, hides the books there and calls in an alarm from a public telephone. With nowhere to go he finally runs to Faber's house.
There he informs the old professor about everything that has happened and confesses that he doesn't know what to do next. He apologizes for putting Faber into danger by coming to his house, but the professor does not mind. He even thanks Montag for making him feel alive again. Faber outlines an escape plan to him, telling him to follow the river down to some old railroad tracks and walk along them. There he might discover "walking camps" (p. 170) full of academics ("old Harvard degrees", ibid.) and find shelter with them. Faber himself plans to go to St. Louis and try and find a retired printer who might print books. Before Montag takes off, they turn on Faber's TV set for news. They learn that another Hound has been dispatched to locate and kill Montag. To mislead the Hound Montag takes Faber's oldest and dirtiest clothes and instructs him to clean his flat with alcohol so that the Hound will not be able to detect any traces.
Montag leaves Faber's apartment and makes towards the river as instructed. On his way he stops to peer into a house to see how the search for him is progressing. The citizens watching the action on their walls and the listeners hearing it on their ear shells are asked, by the announcer, to actively participate in the search for Montag. Everyone is urged to join together and step out of their doors and scan the area around their houses. "At the count of ten now! *One! Two!*" (p. 178) the announcer shouts. Montag himself listens on his own ear shell as the countdown progresses. It propels him to run faster. He makes it to the river where he drops his clothes and puts on Faber's dirty clothing before floating off down the river. He is soon able to touch the ground and reach the river bank. Smells of hay and the motion of the waters bring back childhood memories: Montag fantasizes about sleeping on a bed of warm, dry hay and awaking to a cool glass of milk. His daydream is interrupted when a deer nearby is moving about. Montag is immediately alert, believing at first the Hound has found him.
He walks until he hits the train tracks which he follows as Faber had instructed him to do. After about half an hour he sees a fire some distance away. He walks towards the fire and there he finds a group of elder men who are engaged in discussion. To his surprise Montag is addressed by his name by the group's unofficial leader, Granger, who invites him to join the group. Granger

tells him that they have been following the search for Montag on their small portable TV. In order to mask his body scent so that the Hound cannot smell him Montag is given a special drink that will change his chemical balance. Together the men watch TV. They see how the Hound catches a man and kills him. The TV announcer says that the person caught and killed has been Montag so that the search ends. As the representatives of the state the police and the announcer cannot admit that Montag has managed to escape. An innocent person has been misused as as target so that the public is made aware of the efficiency of the system: "a crime against society has been avenged" (p. 192), as the announcer puts it.
Granger then introduces the badly shaken Montag to the other men. They are all old professionals, authors, university professors, clergymen who are hiding outside the city to avoid being imprisoned. Each of them, so Montag is informed, has memorized a book, a classic of literature, philosophy or a book of the Bible, so that mankind's cultural heritage will not disappear. In the words of Granger: "We're not out to incite or anger anyone yet. For if we are destroyed, the knowledge is dead, perhaps for good. We are model citizens, in our own special way; we walk the old tracks, we lie in the hills at night, and the city people let us be." (p. 195) Montag learns that there are literally "thousands" of them that will pass their knowledge on until the time comes when mankind is again ready to read books.
The next morning the group of men witness the total destruction of the city by enemy bombers. Montag is unmoved when he realizes that Mildred has most likely died in the inferno. At this point he finally remembers where he met his wife – in Chicago. Later the men prepare a breakfast. While they are frying some bacon Granger compares society to the mythical phoenix and points out how that bird continually burned itself and was reborn, only to make the same mistake again. The reference to the cycle of death and rebirth provides the novel with an optimistic ending. What is more, as the men walk towards the destroyed city there is some hope that they might indeed manage to rebuild society.

The Characters

Montag's Development

At the outset, the novel's protagonist Guy Montag is described as a fireman who takes pride in his work, and who is close to being a pyromaniac. He thoroughly identifies with his job, his face displays a permanent "fiery smile" (p. 10) and to him "[k]erosene is nothing but perfume" (p. 13). He has been a fireman for ten years, loyal to the state and his superior, never questioning what he does and why he is ordered to do it. To him burning books "is fine work" (p. 15). It is only when he meets his teenage neighbour, the almost seventeen-year-old Clarisse, that things begin to change. Her questioning him – "Are you happy?" – triggers off the realization that "he was not happy" (p. 20), and, what is more, deprives him of his social persona: "He wore his happiness like a mask and the girl had run off across the lawn with the mask and there was no way of going to knock on her door and ask for it back." (ibid.)

The second encounter with Clarisse sets in motion an even stronger emotion. After Clarisse has told him: "[...] it's so strange you're a fireman, it just doesn't seem right for you, somehow" (p. 34), Montag begins to experience a growing alienation from both his wife and his job. He realizes that there is "a wall between him and Mildred [...]. Literally not just one wall but, so far, three" (p. 59) and starts to see the TV programmes critically. Commenting on one of the shows Mildred is watching he says: "Who *are* these people? Who's that man and who's that woman? Are they husband and wife, are they divorced, engaged, what? Good God, *nothing's* connected up." (p. 61) Montag here anticipates almost verbatim the ideas expressed by media critic Neil Postman 32 years later in his bestselling book *Amusing Ourselves to Death* where he spoke of decontextualized information and concluded that we live in a peek-a-boo world, "where now this event, now that, pops into view for a moment, then vanishes again. It is a world without much coherence or sense; a world that does not ask us, indeed, does not permit us to do anything; a world that is, like the child's game of peek-a-boo, entirely self-contained." (Postman, 1985, p. 77)

With regard to his job, the Hound threatens Montag for the first time, and he observes that "there were vague stirrings of unease in him" (p. 44). He begins to feel guilty (cf. p. 45) without knowing why. His alienation is made complete after the incident with the old woman whose books and house the firemen burnt down. She has startled Montag by quoting Hugh Latimer's famous words to Nicholas Ridley as they were being burned alive for their unorthodox views in the sixteenth century: "We shall this day light such a candle, by God's grace, in England, as I trust shall never be put out [...]." (p. 54)

Like Latimer and Ridley, the old woman burns to death rather than sacrifice her views and her books. Returning home from his job he ponders on his having secretly snatched a book: "So it was the hand that started it all. He felt one hand and then the other work his coat free and let it slump to the floor. He held his pants out into an abyss and let them fall into darkness. His hands had been infected, and soon it would be his arms. He could feel the poison working up his wrists and into his elbows and his shoulders, and then the jump-over from shoulder-blade to shoulder-blade like a spark leaping a gap. His hands were ravenous. And his eyes were beginning to feel hunger, as if they must look at something, anything, everything." (pp. 55 f) The quoted passage suggests that Montag's illness will have a positive effect and may even strengthen him. This becomes even more obvious when Montag who has "never been sick before" (p. 65) develops a fever and becomes sick: "[...] suddenly the odour of kerosene made him vomit." (p. 66) Set against the earlier description that kerosene was like a perfume to him his sickness here signals a clear change in his mental state as it symbolically cleanses him and will ultimately leave him in a higher and enhanced state of mental health.
Before Montag can begin to read in earnest he is visited by his superior Captain Beatty who lectures him about the history of the firemen and the social philosophy of the state. After Beatty has left, Montag begins to feel a growing sense of dissatisfaction with his job. Recalling the incident in which the old woman was burnt he muses: "[...] and I suddenly realized I didn't like [the firemen] at all, and I didn't like myself at all any more." (p. 87)
It becomes clear at this point that he has lost the centre of his life and that his job no longer provides him with a meaningful design. The once committed fireman for whom it was a pleasure to burn has become a morose, deeply troubled man who is racked by self-doubts.
Lured by the books he has illegally acquired Montag begins to read and forces his wife Mildred to join him in his reading. When she protests asking: "Why should I read? What *for*?" (p. 95), he fails to convince her of the humanistic value of reading. In his frustration he remembers the old Professor Faber, the only educated person he knows and calls him. This move is another indicator of Montag's distancing himself from his job as a fireman. He pleads with Faber to help him: "You're the only one I knew might help me. To see." (p. 106) Asked by Faber why he is so badly shaken Montag replies: "We have everything we need to be happy, but we aren't happy. Something's missing. I looked around. The only thing I positively *knew* was gone was the books I'd burned in ten or twelve years. So I thought books might help." (p. 107) Just as Captain Beatty lectured Montag on the need for burning books, Faber lectures him on their value. His ideas prompt Montag to develop subversive ideas, to become a dissident who seeks to fight the system by putting books in firemen's houses, thus sowing the "seeds of suspicion [...] among these arsonists" (p. 111). Faber agrees to help him and promises to see an old

printer who might do reprints. Furthermore, he provides Montag with an electronic device which he wears inside his ear. This device works as a two-way radio, which enables the two to communicate over long distances. Hence Faber will act as a kind of mentor who will help Montag in his dealings with Captain Beatty: "I'll give you things to say." (p. 118)
The encounter with Faber influences Montag in two ways. First he displays open rebelliousness by making the two lady friends of his wife listen to the poem he reads to them. This act clearly constitutes a violation of society's laws. Secondly, listening to the old man's voice in the following days and nights, Montag's imagination produces a new state of self-awareness:

> "Now he knew that he was two people, that he was above all Montag, who knew nothing, who did not even know himself a fool, but only suspected it. And he knew that he was also the old man who talked to him […] assured him, promised him. He would be Montag-plus-Faber, fire plus water, and then, one day, after everything had mixed and simmered and worked away in silence, there would be neither fire nor water, but wine. Out of two separate and opposite things, a third. And one day he would look back upon the fool and know the fool. Even now he could feel the start of the long journey, the leave-taking, the going away from the self he had been." (p. 133)

In his reverie Montag imagines that fire and water, Faber and himself will combine to form a new substance, a new self, here symbolized by wine. This reverie enables him to believe in his own value again which, significantly, has nothing to do with his being a fireman any more. Rather, the reverie in question and others to follow signal a complete revaluation of his view of life. Montag develops a desire for some kind of instinctive perception of nature and knowledge about the earth that are explored in detail at the end of Part 3. The most important reverie comes about when Montag, after having set aflame his house and having killed Beatty, escapes from the city and is floating in the river. He experiences "a sudden peacefulness, away from the city and the lights and the chase, away from everything. He felt as if he had left a stage behind and many actors. […] He was moving from an unreality that was frightening into a reality that was unreal because it was new." (p. 180) Floating leisurely Montag begins to contemplate:

> "The sun burned every day. It burnt Time. The world rushed in a circle and turned on its axis and time was busy burning the years and the people anyway, without help from him. So if *he* burnt things with the firemen and the sun burnt Time, that meant *everything* burned!
> One of them had to stop burning. The sun wouldn't, certainly. So it looked as if it had to be Montag and the people he had worked with until a few short hours ago." (p. 181)

This key passage illuminates Montag's need for some form of permanence to counteract the instability of destruction and change. His emerging desire aims at something enduring in his existence – history, heritage, culture. Montag seeks, in essence then, a definition and a preservation of individual identity and of civilization in general. Thus he vows never to burn anything again. This is an affirmation that stands in marked contrast to everything that Beatty has stood for. After this reverie, in which he interprets his life backward and forward in time, he emerges from the river a happy man, discovering in delight the abundance and richness of the earth's odours: "He stood breathing, and the more he breathed the land in, the more he was filled up with all the details of the land. He was not empty. There was more than enough here to fill him." (p. 186) He goes on to walk through a forest in which he imagines himself an animal, "a thing of brush and liquid eye" (p. 187), until he finds the campfire of the book people. The fire is a complete reversal of the values previously associated with fire, as it is warming instead of being destructive. After he has joined the group and become one its members, Montag is given a new purpose in life. He is told that the book he has memorized with the help of Faber is now what he will be. Hence he is now leaving behind his fireman persona for good by becoming the *Book of Ecclesiastes* (a book of the Old Testament written in the person of Solomon).

The stages of Montag's development may be summarized as follows:

- The first part of the novel shows a hero who is initially proud of being a fireman, then, due to his encounters with Clarisse, starts to question himself and becomes sick after he witnessed the death of the old woman.
- He starts to dissociate himself from his work as a fireman and begins to have rebellious thoughts.
- He turns to Faber as his spiritual guide and begins to behave subversively.
- He kills Beatty and escapes from the city to the wilderness.
- He revaluates his life, discovers the significance of nature and no longer needs an outside authority to give his life a new meaning.
- Thus he has moved from the nihilistic, life-denying role of fireman to a life-affirming man who finally quotes St. John's words from *The Revelations* (the last book of the New Testament, the Apocalypse) about the tree of life rooted now in this world.

The Relationship Montag – Clarisse

Montag meets the 17-year-old girl who is new in his neighbourhood three times. When he sees her for the first time, the girl is introduced in this way:

> "Her face was slender and milk-white, and in it was a kind of gentle hunger that touched over everything with tireless curiosity. It was a look, almost, of pale surprise; the dark eyes were so fixed to the world that no move escaped them. Her dress was white and it whispered. He almost thought he heard the motion of her hands as she walked, and the infinitely small sound now, the white stir of her face turning when she discovered she was a moment away from a man who stood in the middle of the pavement waiting." (p. 12)

From the very beginning Clarisse is associated with whiteness whilst Montag is singed and blackened by his own flames, "a minstrel man, burnt-corked" (p. 10), whose burning of books has even made the "wind turned dark with burning" (ibid.). The antithetical introduction of the two characters is initially given shape by the contrasting use of colours. Montag's darkness represents the ignorance and emptiness of his mind which has been rendered blank by his job as a fireman. The whiteness associated with Clarisse signals, in contrast, her mental brightness and imagination. In terms of colour symbolism, white, which is usually considered to be the presence of all colour, confronts dark, the absence of all colour. Clarisse is, as it turns out, not only a very observant person, she is also imaginative and a lover of nature. Her liveliness and inner warmth is underlined by the following perception: "Her face, turned to him now, was fragile milk crystal with a soft and constant light in it. It was not the hysterical light of electricity but – what? But the strangely comfortable and rare and gently flattering light of the candle." (p. 14) Clarisse's inquisitiveness, her concern about fellow beings as well as her non-conformist behaviour leave Montag greatly unsettled. Unlike him she notices that "[t]here's dew on the grass in the morning" (p. 16) which illustrates her closeness to nature. With her final question – "Are you happy?" (p. 17) – she confronts Montag with his own ego's identification with his social role. Montag's reaction after she has left – "Happy! Of all the nonsense" (ibid.) – illustrates that Clarisse has awakened him from his mental apathy. The following lines show the impact Clarisse has made on him:

> "Montag shook his head. He looked at a blank wall. The girl's face was there, really quite beautiful in memory: astonishing, in fact. She had a very thin face like the dial of a small clock in the middle of a night when you waken to see the time and see the clock telling you the hour and the minute and the second, with a white silence and a glowing, all certainty and knowing what it has to tell of the night passing swiftly on toward further darknesses but moving also toward a new sun." (p. 18)

In figurative language Clarisse's role for Montag is foreshadowed here. Just as the dial of the clock informs you about the time and thus provides you with some sort of orientation, Clarisse will illuminate Montag's development.

Their contrasting roles could be summarized like this:

Clarisse

- associated with whiteness
- observant person
- lover of nature
- remembers the past
- lives in a world of communication and imagination

Montag

- associated with darkness
- unimaginative
- has no links to the past
- lives in a world of isolation and destruction

Clarisse's role becomes more obvious during their second encounter. In the dandelion episode (cf. pp. 32 f) she reveals to Montag that he really does not love anyone, that unhappiness is his true state of being. Hence she confronts him with his stale and loveless life. Furthermore, mention is made of her non-conformist behaviour. Clarisse confesses to Montag that she regularly has to see a psychiatrist. Her deviance from standard social norms – "the psychiatrist wants to know why I go out and hike around in the forests and watch the birds and collect butterflies" (p. 33) – makes her a social outcast. It should be noted that her deviant behaviour is again an expression of the technique of reversal: behaviour that is completely acceptable in our society has become a sign of mental disturbance.

When they meet for the third time Clarisse assumes the role of social critic: "[...] we never ask questions, or at least most don't; they just run the answers at you, bing, bing, bing, [...]. That's not social to me at all. It's a lot of funnels and a lot of water poured down the spout and out of the bottom, and them telling us it's wine when it's not. They run us so ragged by the end of the day we can't do anything but go to bed or head for a Fun Park to bully people around, break window panes in the Window Smasher place or wreck cars in the Car Wrecker place with the big steel ball." (pp. 41 f)

Clarisse's criticism refers to two different aspects. Firstly, she speaks out against the brainwashing done by society's power structure. The perception of reality has been manipulated to such an extent that people only perceive what they are meant to perceive. In other words, all individual critical faculties have been suspended. Secondly, there are government-induced forms of controlled aggression which serve as a kind of safety-valve. By being able to act out their aggressive feelings in leisure activities people indulge in games rather than turn their aggressive potential against the government. Clarisse's speech resembles a personal revelation: she enumerates various activities that underline her critical attitude.

The three encounters and Clarisse's function may be summarized as follows:

- First encounter: Clarisse confronts Montag with his ego and awakens him from his mental apathy.
- Second encounter: She confronts him with his loveless life.
- Third encounter: She confronts him with the meaninglessness of his life.
- Clarisse's function: She provides Montag with new insights by connecting him to the past and by showing him alternative ways of thinking and living; she sets in motion his search for identity and she acts as his mentor.

The Relationship Montag – Mildred

When Montag enters his bedroom after his disturbing first encounter with Clarisse, he finds "[c]omplete darkness, not a hint of the silver world outside, the windows tightly shut, the chamber a tomb-world where no sound from the great city could penetrate" (p. 19). The darkness is that of a mausoleum, the deathly milieu of the TV "family" and the ear radio in which Mildred figuratively entombs herself. The opening description thus illustrates her spiritual death and makes it clear that she is the exact opposite of a self-determined individual:

> "[...] an electronic ocean of sound, of music and talk and music and talk coming in, coming in on the shore of her unsleeping mind. The room was indeed empty. Every night the waves came in and bore her off on their great tides of sound, floating her, wide-eyed, toward morning. There had been no night in the last two years that Mildred had not swum that sea, had not gladly gone down in it for the third time." (p. 20)

By constantly seeking distraction Mildred attempts to hide her emptiness by various forms of artificial intoxication. Thus she immerses herself in every technological gadget available to her which allow her a continuous escape from reality. And if she isn't doing just that her utterances resemble the sounds and word patterns of a young child: "She talked to him for what seemed a long while and she talked about this and she talked about that and it was only words, like the words he had heard once in a nursery at a friend's house, a two-year-old child building word patterns, talking jargon, making pretty sounds in the air." (p. 56)

Unlike Clarisse Mildred displays no intellectual curiosity whatsoever, she is devoid of any form of imagination. She is completely consumer-minded and possesses a blind narcissistic enthusiasm for identifying with "exotic people's lives". That is why she insists to have a fourth TV wall installed: "If we had a fourth wall, why it'd be just like this room wasn't ours at all, but all kinds of exotic people's rooms" (p. 31), that is why she mindlessly consumes the electronic and visual products of a standardized mass culture. Thus it will come as no surprise that their marriage is completely estranged: there is no genuine communication between the two partners, much less any form of togetherness or even intimacy. Significantly Mildred when asked about their first meeting does not remember and dismisses her husband's question as irrelevant: "It doesn't matter." (p. 58) Having eliminated the past completely from her life and her memories, Mildred's centre of attention is exclusively on the here and now, on instant wish-fulfillment and gratification.

The differences between husband and wife become further apparent when Montag confesses to her that he has brought home some books and starts to read to her:

> "Mildred kicked at a book. 'Books aren't people. You read and I look around, but there isn't *anybody*!'
> He stared at the parlour that was dead and grey as the waters of an ocean that might teem with life if they switched on the electronic sun.
> 'Now,' said Mildred, 'my family is people. They tell me things; *I* laugh, they *laugh*!'"
> (p. 95)

These lines make it clear that Mildred has been so conditioned, if not brainwashed, by her electronic experiences that she feels comfortable only in the ersatz world that TV provides for her. Hence she calls the TV characters her "family".

Bradbury has likened the entertainment spewing without end out of the multi-walled TV parlour to "an eruption of Vesuvius". Mildred's lady friends, Mrs Bowles and Mrs Phelps, arrive at Montag's house to watch the White Clowns. With their "Cheshire Cat smiles burning through the walls of the house," they vanish "into the volcano's mouth" (p. 121). The imagery conveys a sense of the ladies' immersion in a wash of lava; they are already burned alive like the citizens of Pompeii, under the ashes of the volcano. If this imagery is linked to the cluster of images used at the beginning – darkness, tomb, mausoleum – it becomes clear that Mildred Montag, the very epitome of *Fahrenheit 451*'s shallow society, has always been an emotionally, spriritually and intellectually dead person.

The major aspects of Mildred's character and outlook on life may be summarized as follows:

- She has no genuine concern for her husband, is only interested in her TV family.
- She has no recollection of their mutual past, lives only in the present.
- She ignores anything unpleasant or intellectually demanding by constantly using the TV as a form of intoxication.
- Deep down she is empty, insensitive and uncaring.
- Mentally she resembles a small child as can be seen by her senseless babbling.
- Having no interests other than her TV family she is incapable of having any real communication.

Captain Beatty: The Representative of the System

As Montag has called in sick at the fire station his superior Captain Beatty decides to pay him a visit, correctly assuming that Montag is facing a psychological crisis on account of his latest action as a fireman. When Beatty comes into Montag's house, he immediately takes charge of the household, telling Mrs Montag to turn the TV off. She complies with Beatty's order at once, a fact which stands in marked contrast to her refusal to switch it off when asked by Montag the previous evening. Beatty then slips into the role of a solicitous superior expressing understanding for Montag's state of mind: "Every fireman, sooner or later, hits this. They only need understanding, to know how the wheels run." (p. 71) What follows is a detailed lecture about the history of the firemen, a sociological treatise on the decline of book reading and a summary of the philosophical foundation of the society they live in. Throughout his whole explanations Beatty's role is that of master who lectures his disciple. Hence Montag is reduced to a mere sounding-board, stating his occasional agreement when asked. The conversation between him and Beatty is by no means a debate in which two intellectual and equal partners discuss something, rather it serves a didactic function as it explains the ideology of this future society.

Beatty begins his lecture with a brief historical overview of the firemen's job: "When did it all start, you ask, this job of ours, how did it come about, where, when?" (ibid.) He seems to refrain from using "why", thus leaving out any reference as to why the firemen came into being. He dates the origin of their profession to an unspecified Civil War and links it then to the beginning of mass production in popular culture.

According to Beatty, the trend leading up to the disuse of books got started when modern technology, beginning with photography, enabled communication "to have *mass*" (ibid.). The use of "mass" refers here to the greater amount of information carried. Whereras earlier oral and printed forms of communication still left much information to the imagination of the audience, moving pictures shifted this "mass" from the audience to the means of communication themselves. Rather than challenge audiences, controllers of communication chose to rely on "mass" to sell, thereby simplifying the ideas being transmitted:

> "And because they had mass, they became simpler [...]. Once, books appealed to a few people, here, there, everywhere. They could afford to be different. The world was roomy. But then the world got full of eyes and elbows and mouths. Double, triple, quadruple population. Films and radios, magazines, books levelled down to a sort of paste pudding norm" (pp. 71f).

The metaphor of the "paste pudding" refers to a reduction of communication. In keeping with the imagery, forms of public communication have been emptied of any conflicting, thought-provoking content.

Interestingly, Beatty links the decline of thought to the public's desire to avoid controversy in favour of mere entertainment. The "publishers, exploiters, broadcasters" are not, as one might suppose, the conscious manipulators of the public. Instead, as controllers of mass communication they only convert the public's desire for pleasure into practice: "Whirl man's mind around about so fast [...] that the centrifuge flings off all unnecessary, time-wasting thought." (p. 73) Knowing that the public prefers inconsequentialities and trivialities over contemplation and evaluation, the exploiters "empty the

theatres save for clowns and furnish the rooms with glass walls and pretty colours running up and down the walls like confetti or blood or sherry or sauterne" (p. 74). Beatty's imagery here clearly mirrors the contents of the four-wall televisions with its triviality ("confetti"), violence ("blood") and intoxication ("sherry or sauterne").
Although the exploiters bear most of the responsibility for the decline of thought, the exploited are at least as guilty, for they are willingly exploited. Thus Beatty notes that the public "knowing what it want[s], spin[s] happily" and he goes on to say to Montag: "Ask yourself, what do we want in this country, above all? People want to be happy, isn't that right? [...] I want to be happy, people say. Well, aren't they? Don't we keep them moving, don't we give them fun? That's all we live for, isn't it? For pleasure, for titillation? And you must admit our culture provides plenty of these." (p. 78)
The rationale behind Beatty's thoughts is egalitarianism and hedonism. Having been made alike and conditioned to even the least attractive things that television presents, the public has become accustomed to enjoying mindless mass communication. The masses have become, as it were, both unable and unwilling to break with conformity. As Bradbury himself points out in his *Afterword to the 2008 edition* in which he voices his criticism of excessive media consumption and mass exploitation: "[...] you don't have to burn books, do you, if the world starts to fill up with non-readers, non-learners, non-knowers? If the world widescreen basketballs and footballs itself to drown in MTV, no Beattys are needed to ignite the kerosene or hunt the reader." (pp. 225 f)
A second strand of Beatty's sociological treatise refers to his depiction of the role of intolerant minority groups. As he explains to Montag in the past intolerant pressure groups were influential in stifling free expression and fostering conformity that eventually allowed the government to begin its own censoring:

> "Bigger the population, the more minorities. Don't step on the toes of the dog-lovers, cat-lovers, doctors, lawyers, merchants, chiefs, Mormons, Baptists, Unitarians, second-generation Chinese, Swedes, Italians, Germans, Texans, Brooklynites, Irishmen, people from Oregon or Mexico. The people in this book, this play, this TV serial are not meant to represent any actual painters, cartographers, mechanics anywhere. The bigger your market, Montag, the less you handle controversy, remember that! All the minor minor minorities with their navels to be kept clean. Authors, full of evil thoughts, lock up your typewriters. They *did*. Magazine became a nice blend of vanilla tapioca. Books [...] were dishwater." (pp. 75 f)

Beatty here directly claims minority pressure as a cause of intellectual self-censorship and conformity, hence carrying the idea of political correctness to bizarre extremes. He concludes this part of his lecture by emphasizing that books stopped selling because of the public's desire for easy gratification: "There you have it, Montag. It didn't come from the Government down. There was no dictum, no declaration, no censorhip, to start with, no!

Technology, mass exploitation, and minority pressure carried the trick. Today, thanks to them, you can stay happy all the time, you are allowed to read comics, the good old confessions, or trade-journals." (p. 76)
By taking a close look at the way Beatty presents his ideas and the language he employs several characteristics that feature throughout the whole lecture become clear. To begin with, the captain mainly uses short, declarative sentences. There are virtually no conjunctions, the captain speaks in strings of main clauses. The absence of conjunctions indicates that he obviously feels no need to argue, much less to justify anything. Instead he enumerates, hammering away his statements and facts, thus seeking to convince Montag by the sheer quantity of the information given. Additionally, he avails himself of a series of rhetorical questions which are meant to elicit the listener's consent as, for example, in the quote given above in which mention is made of the pleasure principle. Occasionally, Beatty also uses striking metaphors and euphemisms. For instance, he emphasizes the danger of possessing a book by calling it "a loaded gun " (p. 77) and plays down the process by which books have become problem-free as a "paste pudding norm" (p. 72). Thus it becomes apparent that the captain is an utter cynic and nihilist who does not recognize any values or moral standards nor does he seek any new ones. To him, life is devoid of any meaning, it is essentially empty: "Life is immediate, the job counts, pleasure lies all about after work. Why learn anything save pressing buttons, pulling switches, fitting nuts and bolts? [...] Life becomes one big pratfall, Montag; everything bang, boff, and wow!" (pp. 73 f)
When Montag returns to work the captain tells him of a dream of beatitude. His dream takes the form of a rhetorical battle of citations, with Montag trying tro defend the integrity and ideal meaning of literature and Beatty taking the opposite tactic by quoting the books against themselves, thus displaying his interpretative power over the text of his dream. By showing Montag that books can contradict themselves, Beatty apparently wins the battle and seems to stand on the side of reason. The dream ends with Montag climbing on board the fire engine with Beatty. Both of them drive "back to the firehouse in beatific silence, all dwindled away to peace" (p. 139). In reality, however, they drive off to burn Montag's own house, for Mildred has put in the alarm. When Beatty deliberately provokes Montag into killing him with the flame-thrower, Montag realizes that his superior wants to die. Beatty, then, is ultimately a person who is satisfied with meaninglessness and who is content with the fact that for him there is no answer to the question "What for?" and "Why?"

Faber: The Critic of the System

After Captain's Beatty's lecture and Mildred's unresponsiveness to his needs to learn more about books Montag wonders: "[...] where do you get help, where do you find a teacher this late?" (p. 97) and remembers the old Professor Faber whom he met a year ago. Wanting to secure the Bible he took from the old woman's house – "[i]t might be the last copy in this part of the world" (p. 99) – he calls Faber and asks him how many copies of the Bible are left in the country. Faber is unwilling to speak on the phone, years of fear have made him more distrusting than ever and he promptly hangs up on Montag. Montag, on some level, realizes that if he has to turn a book in to Beatty, he does not want it to be the one that is precious and might soon be lost to the world. Upon contemplating this he leaves his house and takes the subway to Faber's.

When Montag turns up on Faber's doorstep the old man is afraid, but his obvious reverence for the fact that Montag is holding one of the last copies of the Bible under his arm outweighs his fear and he invites him in. He asks Montag to give him the book, and although he states that he is not a religious man, he realizes that the value of the text which stands for the history of Christianity and of humanity cannot be denied. Faber then smells the Bible in his hands: "Do you know that books smell like nutmeg or some spice from a foreign land? I loved to smell them when I was a boy." (p. 106) He then confesses to having been a "coward: I saw the way things were going, a long time back. I said nothing. I'm one of the innocents who could have spoken up and out when no one would listen to the 'guilty', but I did not speak and thus became guilty myself." (ibid.) Faber's own words mark him as a fellow traveller who remained silent when outspokenness and public criticism were needed. Similar to Beatty, Faber begins to lecture Montag. His lecture however focusses on the value of books and is not meant to indoctrinate Montag. Instead, Faber wants to share his ideas with his disciple. Within the framework of the relationships between the central characters of the novel Faber then assumes the role of the intellectual antagonist to Beatty.

Responding to Montag's outcry that people aren't happy Faber names three things that are missing in the dystopian society: quality, leisure and the right to act on the ground of what is learned from these things. When speaking about the former function of books in society Faber declares:

> "It's not books you need, it's some of the things that once were in books. The same things *could* be in the 'parlour families' today. The same infinite detail and awareness could be projected through the radios and televisors, but are not. No, no, it's not books at all you're looking for! Take it where you can find it, in old phonograph records, old motion pictures, and in old friends; look for it in nature and look for it in yourself. Books were only one type of receptacle where we stored a lot of things we were afraid we might forget. There is nothing magical in them at all. The magic is only in what books say, how they stitched the patches of the universe into one garment for us." (pp. 107f)

The metaphor of the "garment" clearly alludes to the former role of literature to "stitch the patches of the universe together". Faber then expands

upon this idea by comparing books to "pores": "Do you know why books such as this are so important? Because they have quality. [...] To me it means texture. This book has *pores*." (p. 108) The metaphor of the pores refers to Faber's view of what constitutes literature. According to him, books confront the reader with deep imaginative experiences and a completeness of information that the soaps or TV families in their society no longer provide. However, to be able to enjoy this "texture" man must have "leisure" which Faber defines as having "time to think" (p. 109). Leisure suggests freedom from routine and continuous TV consumerism, it implies the freedom to determine one's own activities. Therefore Faber concludes: "[...] you can't argue with the four-wall televisor. Why? The televisor is 'real'. It is immediate, it has dimension. It tells you what to think and blasts it in. It *must* be right. It *seems* so right. It rushes you on so quickly to its own conclusions your mind hasn't time to protest [...]." (ibid.)
By reading and having at the same time leisure man is enabled "to carry out actions based on what we learn from the interaction of the first two" (p. 110). The enlightening quality inherent in literature and, by extension, in reading is seen as indispensible for leading a mature, self-determined existence. Faber's ideas are illustrated in Outline 4 on p. 71 of this study aid.

Beatty ⟷ **Faber**

Antagonists

Beatty	Faber
• man in a blue shirt with an orange snake stitched to it	• associated with whiteness
• Montag's superior	• Montag's mentor
• advocate of egalitarianism	• advocate of enlightenment, of knowledge and reason, of individual self-determination
• nihilist, cynic	• believer in man's ability to learn and grow intellectually and in human virtues
• dystopian functionary: enforcer of the totalitarian system	• silent dissident turning active
• provokes his own death	• fate unknown: probably dies in the nuclear inferno

Throughout their conversation Montag is the one who wishes to change the hopelessness of the situation by taking action. His idea is to begin making copies of the books they already have so that they won't be lost forever for future generations. Faber is shocked by this idea which he considers too risky and jokingly tells Montag it would be better to burn down the fire-houses themselves or print extra books to hide in the firemen's houses to implicate them. However, Montag takes this seriously and jumps on the idea. Faber grows excited by Montag's fierce commitment, but then starts to doubt the feasibility of his plan and tells Montag to go home and enjoy what little life time is left to him before the war bombs will kill him and everyone else. This is the point where Montag uses Faber's reverence for the Bible to black-mail his fear out of him and prompt him to help. Faber then shows Montag the electronic transmitter he built and offers to assist, from a distance, by being Montag's audio guide, thus helping him to deal with Beatty in their upcoming confrontation. From this point onwards it becomes clear that Faber is now the antagonist of Beatty. Their respective roles and positions are juxtaposed in the table on p. 37 of this study aid.

After Montag has killed Beatty he returns to Faber's house. Faber tells him that he feels alive for the first time in years and thanks Montag for sparking in him the desire to take action again and helping him to not be afraid. Faber informs him about his plans to go to St. Louis to see a retired printer there. After that they part, and it remains unclear whether he will survive the nuclear devastation. The very fact that he literally drops out of the plot signals his didactic function within the constellation of the central characters. At this point of the story he has fulfilled his role as mentor to Montag and intellectual adversary to Beatty. (For a complete overview of the relationships between the central characters and their respective functions with regard to Montag see Outline 5 on p. 72 of this study aid.)

The Richness of Imagery: Major Symbols and Motifs

As the opening of the novel indicates, Bradbury uses a style that is rich in imagery. Of the many different symbols that permeate the whole novel three are already introduced in the novel's first paragraph:

> "With the brass nozzle in his fists, with this great python spitting its venomous kerosene upon the world, the blood pounded in his head, and his hands were the hands of some amazing conductor playing all the symphonies of blazing and burning [...]. He wanted above all [...] to shove a marshmallow on a stick in the furnace, while the flapping pigeon-winged books died on the porch and lawn of the house." (pp. 9 f)

The narrator describes Montag's hands with almost ironic majesty. Montag does not as yet recognize the true nature of his profession, which means destruction; indeed, he finds it "a pleasure to burn." His conscience is at this stage virtually blank, and his self-confident, self-aggrandizing hands reflect this state of blankness and emptiness. But after having taking books from the forbidden libraries Montag's hands reflect the unacknowledged dictates of conscience:

> "A book alighted [...] like a white pigeon, in his hands, wings fluttering. [...]
> Montag's hand closed like a mouth, crushed the book with wild devotion, with an insanity of mindlessness to his chest. [...]
> Montag had done nothing. His hand had done it all, his hand with a brain of its own, with a conscience and a curiosity in each trembling finger, had turned thief. Now, it plunged the book back under his arm, pressed it tight to sweating armpit, rushed out empty [...].
> He gazed, shaken, at that white hand." (p. 51)

Here, a direct link is established between Montag's conscience and his hands. His hands are, of course, not possessed by "an insanity of mindlessness", but as Montag is still unwilling to accept that he has "a conscience and a curiosity" he projects them onto his hands.
During his first visit at Faber's Montag holds out the Bible he has brought with him: "Montag stood there and waited for the next thing to happen. His hands, by themselves, like two men working together, began to rip the pages from the book. The hands tore the fly-leaf and then the first and then the second page. [...] Montag [...] let his hands continue." (p. 114)
Again Montag's hands express what his consciousness can scarcely recognize. He has no real wish to damage, much less destroy the old Bible, but subconsciously he apparently understands that Faber's help is even more important. Once he returns to the firehouse, his hands feel restless under the gaze of Captain Beatty:

> "In Beatty's sight, Montag felt the guilt of his hands. His fingers were like ferrets that had done some evil [...]. If Beatty so much as breathed on them, Montag felt that his

> hands might wither, turn over on their sides, and never be shocked to life again; they would be buried the rest of his life in his coat-sleeves, forgotten. For those were the hands that had acted on their own, no part of him, here was where the conscience first manifested itself to snatch books [...] and now, in the firehouse, these hands seemed gloved with blood." (p. 136)

Though Montag still has trouble accepting responsibility for breaking away from his way of life as a fireman, the narrator significantly uses the word "conscience" again. Just as his hands first manifested his new conscience, they now reflect his fear of being discovered. And when he is about to kill Beatty the narrator has again Montag's conscience drive the hands onward before the conscious mind has reasoned out the situation: "Montag [...] glanced to his hands to see what new thing they had done. Thinking back later he could never decide whether the hands or Beatty's reaction to the hands gave him the final push toward murder." (p. 154)

When Montag escapes into the wilderness and joins the book people, his first glimpse of them shows only "many hands held to [the campfire's] warmth, hands without arms" (p. 187). After a lengthy conversation with Granger, the group's leader, Montag helps to put out the campfire: "The other men helped, and Montag helped, and there, in the wilderness, the men all moved their hands, putting out the fire together." (p. 197) Putting out the fire in this context is certainly a symbolic act, signalling the end of the book-burnings, but the explicit mentioning of hands seems equally symbolic, for now the hands are seen as a force doing good. The various descriptions of Montag's hands throughout the novel thus function as a mirror of his conscience; they represent Montag's spiritual and moral growth and show the extent to which he has become a self-determined individual.

Another important cluster of images refers to animals, notably reptiles and birds. As mentioned above, the brass nozzle with which Montag burns books is both personified and compared to a python. The personification suggests that the man and his action have become one, whilst the use of the snake at this stage signals danger and destruction. The image of the snake is again taken up when the narrator describes the machines the technicians use to pump out Mildred's stomach and replace her blood. The first machine is "like a black cobra" (pp. 22 f) and the second evokes these observations in Montag: "Go on, anyway, shove the bore down, slush up the emptiness, if such a thing could be brought out in the throb of the suction snake" (p. 23). And he wonders if it really "did suck out all the poisons accumulated with the years?" Within the context quoted the snake-like machines act as defenders of the status quo; they do replace Mildred's blood but do not rejuvenate her soul. By extension, then, they are symbols of evil as they do not change a person's sick mental state. – Similarly, the salamander is put to use. It is one of the official symbols of the firemen as well as the name given to their fire engines, thus signalling the destruction that both bring about once they are called upon.

Apart from these animals Bradbury frequently employs birds in connection with books. Throughout the novel books are "pigeon-winged" (e.g. p. 10), like "a white pigeon [...] [with] wings fluttering" (p. 51), "like slaughtered birds" whose pages are like "snowy feathers" (ibid.) and finally "like roasted birds, their wings ablaze with red and yellow feathers" (p. 151). A close examination of the contexts in which this imagery is used reveals that the symbolism is twofold. The first context, the opening paragraph, makes it clear that the poetic image refers to the idea of freedom. Even though the books are destroyed, the ideas behind them live on. This holds true also for the second context. Even though the library of the old woman is destroyed and she herself dies in the fire, her quote stays with Montag and ultimately makes him aware of the fact that there is a real person behind each book. They third context refers to Montag's burning those books he has illegally hidden in his house. Here the imagery seems to suggest that the books are so ablazed that they will inevitably die. Such a reading is certainly corroborated by the novel's ending and notably by the reference to the mythical bird Phoenix:

> "There was a damn silly bird called a Phoenix back before Christ: every few hundred years he built a pyre and burned himself up. He must have been first cousin to Man. But every time he burnt himself up he sprang out of the ashes, he got himself born all over again. And it looks like we're doing the same thing, over and over, but we've got one damn thing the Phoenix never had. We know the damn silly thing we just did. We know all the damn silly things we've done for a thousand years, and as long as we know that and always have it around where we can see it, some day we'll stop making the goddam funeral pyres and jumping into the middle of them." (pp. 208 f)

When Granger compares mankind to the mythical bird shortly after the nuclear inferno in which the city has been annihilated he wants to point out that man's advantage is his ability of reflecting on the mistakes he has made. Hence the symbol of the phoenix that initially served only as an emblem of the firemen expresses a note of optimism. On the one hand, it refers to the cyclical nature of history and the collective rebirth of mankind, and on the other hand it also signals the completion of Montag's spriritual resurrection.

Fahrenheit 451 as Literary Dystopia

Fahrenheit 451 is one of the most famous and popular novels belonging to the literary genre known as dystopias. This term derives from the Greek "Utopia", meaning a "nowhere". Thomas More used the word utopia for the title of his sixteenth-century political novel in which he depicted an ideal and perfect society set in the future. Utopias flourished in the late 19th and early 20th centuries, particularly in the writings of George Herbert Wells. The term "dystopia", by contrast, is used as an antonym of utopia. Hence the future worlds created in these novels usually mirror certain ominous elements of the cultural, social or political reality. Therefore dystopias are warnings, they seek to "prevent", not to "predict" (cf. p. 47 in this study aid) recent negative trends in society.
Most commonly cited as the model of a twentieth-century dystopian novel is the Russian Yevgeny Zamyiatin's *We* (1924), which envisions an oppressive but stable social order. The social stability has been accomplished through the complete extinction of any form of individualism. *We* is usually considered to be the forerunner of George Orwell's *1984* (1948), a nightmarish vision of a totalitarian world in the future. There is censorship involving the rewriting of history, the god-like reverence of the dictator called "Big Brother" and the encouragement of children to spy on and betray their parents. Citizens are treated brutally, torture and murder of dissidents are commonplace. Endless television broadcasts have replaced reading. Television has become a two-way tool, which watches the citizens more intently than the citizens watch it. How this arrangement works is never explained, its plausibility remains questionable.
Unlike *We* and *1984* Aldous Huxley's well-known novel *Brave New World* (1932) makes use of a completely different set of ideas. It depicts a futuristic society in which men and women are genetically programmed, bred in bottles for their designated roles in a strictly hierarchical society. The genetic programming is accompanied by various forms of conditioning, all of which are meant to ensure society's stability and the citizens' happiness. In the words of the Director of the London Hatchery and Conditioning Centre: "That is the secret of happiness and virtue-liking what you have got to do. All conditioning aims at that: making people like their unescapable social destiny." (Huxley, 1994, p. 13) Apart from such means a drug called "soma" is administered to keep the people in a state of happiness. Additionally, social control is enforced among other things by the suppression of literary classics, notably Shakespeare's plays which are considered to be a revolutionary force. As Mustapha Mond, one of the world's controllers, puts it: "You can't make tragedies without social instability. The world's stable now. People are happy; they get what they want, and they never want what they can't get. [...] You've got to choose between happiness and what people used to call high art." (ibid., pp. 200 f)

Huxley's novel introduced a further aspect that has since become part of the genre's convention. In a climactic confrontation between the dissident John Savage and the world controller Mustapha Mond Mond explains to the dissident – and hence to the reader – the state's philosophy. He points out that man no longer needs to exert individual dignity as society has not longer any use for such values or actions. He then goes on to note that society no longer needs to provide man with opportunities of self-realization, as he has been conditioned to instant fulfilment of his needs. Hence man no longer faces the difficulty of having to choose. Rather, everything exists in abundance both in terms of material as well as emotional well-being. Having done away with misfortune and suffering man is not endowed any longer with a conscience, which has indeed become superfluous, as he is no longer facing ethical choices, or as Mond puts it: "Anybody can be virtuous now." (ibid., p. 235) What the controller describes, then, is a carefree way of life, devoid of any obstacles, hardships and even challenges. Captain Beatty almost verbatim repeats the ideas mentioned in the earlier novel.

It is precisely this understanding of happiness which the dissident John Savage vehemently attacks. Refuting Mond's utilitarian view of happiness the Savage claims the right of individual existence. To his mind, such fundamental experiences as "freedom", "goodness" and "sin", all of which include longing, choosing and suffering are necessary for a person to become a mature individual and not be a puppet of chemical and psychological conditioning. Again, the dissident's view is taken up by Clarisse's questioning the validity of Montag's happiness and by the latter's growing dissatisfaction with Beatty's utilitarian outlook on life.

Dystopian conventions are also made use of in John Christopher's book for young readers *The Guardians* (1972). The novel is set in England in the year 2052; the country is made up of two parts: an urban area called Conurbia and a rural part called the County, which is separated from the former by a high wire fence. Life in Conurbia is marked by a never-ending consumption of holovision and various mass sport activities. People indulge in electrocar racing, high-wire combat or simply in rioting after such events. These mass activities represent a safety-valve which the society's ruling oligarchy employs in order to channel man's aggression. Life in Conurbia is thus one-dimensional, devoid of tradition and of any links with the past. Not surprisingly, reading has virtually disappeared, too. The other part of this future England, the County, is a replica of the Edwardian Age prior to World War I. There is a rigid class system, the gentry and their servants. People live in small towns, they do not work but live off investments. Horses are the only means of transport, the overall impression is one of idyllic country life. The social order is truly static and retrograde; no change whatsoever is either desired or tolerated. The social structure is safeguarded either by psychological conditioning or – in case this fails to achieve the desired results – by a group called

the guardians who even though they remain somewhat elusive are reminiscent of a secret police. The guardians crush whatever opposition might develop and see to it that dissidents have to undergo a brain operation which will turn them into well-adjusted, docile persons.
The novel's protagonist is introduced as an individualist from the very beginning. After the death of his father he becomes an orphan and has to attend a boarding school, where he is the only pupil to read and to ask questions in class. He runs away from the school and manages to overcome the wire fence and make it to the County. There he encounters Mike Gifford, a gentry boy, who takes him to his family. The Giffords have Rob pose as the son of a distant cousin and instruct him in the ways of gentry country life. Significantly, Rob's growing integration into the society of the County is paralleled by Mike's increasing rejection of that same society, as he begins to question and to criticize the very foundations of County society. Mike later joins a group of dissidents who start an armed uprising which is soon put down by the guardians. Mike manages to escape, Rob who had refused to take part in the uprising is taken by the guardians for detailed questioning. The guardians' leader, Sir Percy, enlightens Rob about the political structure and seeks to win him as an informant. Rob initially agrees, then has pangs of conscience and makes up his mind to return to the Conurb and try to join a revolutionary group there.
If set against *Fahrenheit 451* a number of similarities emerge. To begin with, there is holovision with its mindless soaps, there is channelled violence and aggression that remind us of the fun parks in Bradbury's novel, where people can smash cars or indulge in similar activities. Furthermore, people are discouraged from reading and any form of intellectual curiosity is considered to be deviant behaviour. And, of course, there is the representative of the system who appears to be a benevolent father figure but who, in reality, is a ruthless defender of society's norms. Speaking about Mike Gifford Sir Percy tells Rob:

> "You're worried about what happens to him? That's understandable. We guardians are not limited by the moralities we lay down for others but I hope we retain human feelings. He will be all right: you have my word for that. A very small operation on the brain, performed by expert surgeons. It won't hurt him. He'll remain active, intelligent, capable of full life. But he won't want to rebel any more. It's a tried and tested technique. We keep it in reserve for cases like this." (Christopher, 1973, pp. 168 f)

In contrast to the dystopian novels mentioned above Ray Bradbury's *Fahrenheit 451* does not picture evil dictator figures like Orwell's O'Brien or dictator-philosophers like Huxley's Mustapha Mond. The crucial difference to these novels lies in the fact that Bradbury does not focus on a ruling elite nor does he portray some kind of higher society. Rather, the novel concentrates on the means of oppression and regimentation that are revealed in the life of an uneducated, complacent working-class fireman. Nonetheless, there are important points of similarities between the three novels. All three describe a technocratic society in which the social order is maintained through oppression and by the total effacement of the individual. Moreover, all three describe a social order accomplished through the banning of books and all three suppress freedom of thought, of press and of self-determination.

Dystopian novels usually have certain structural elements in common. Their main characters are defined in relation to organizational structures. There is, for instance, the defender of the status quo who, if necessary, takes also means to enforce that status. Next, there is an important figure, most often the protagonist, whose growing dissatisfaction with life and whose inner conflicts mirror the inadequacies or defects of the society he lives in. His dissatisfaction is triggered off by a catalyst who acts as his mentor. Apart from this typical constellation of characters there is a group of dissidents who live outside the mainstream society and who represent norms and values that are detrimental to those of the futuristic society. In dystopian novels the way of life of this opposition group is called otherworld. Therefore, a dystopian novel is always made up of a bi-partite structure: the main, futuristic society and the dissident otherworld.

The main society in *Fahrenheit 451* is marked by a complete banning of all books. Reading has been replaced by various forms of mass exploitation such as TV consumerism, mindless activities such as car racing or demolition of objects in special theme parks. Peoples' lives are streamlined, uniformity and conformity have become important social norms. Life has been reduced to simplified entertainment. All sense of the past has been obliterated by the presence of technology, the TV characters and their story lines enable the citizens to create a fictional past and present. Thus people do not understand the importance of the real past in their own lives. For instance, Mildred does not remember, much less care when, where and how she met Guy Montag for the first time.

To some extent, the book people's otherworld as depicted in *Fahrenheit 451* is a reversal of the mainstream society. To begin with, the setting is no longer urban, it is a wilderness that is separated from the city by a river. Here nature is unspoiled as it has been left to itself for ages and it is here that Montag experiences for the first time the variety of smells hitherto unknown to him. Unlike the "great thunderstorm" (p. 60) life in the wilderness is characterized by silence:

> "There was a silence gathered all about that fire and the silence was in the men's faces, and time was there, time enough to sit by this rusting track under the trees, and look at the world and turn it over with the eyes. [...] It was not only the fire that was different. It was the silence. Montag moved toward this special silence that was concerned with all of the world." (pp. 187f)

Silence induces a state of contemplation, of concern with one's surroundings and one's fellow man. It provides you with the idleness or "leisure", as Faber has called it, to develop your own thoughts rather than echo or reply what "the family" has said.

Granger, the group's leader, outlines the purpose of the book people to Montag with these words:

> "We are all bits and pieces of history and literature and international law [...]. All we want to do is keep the knowledge we think we will need, intact and safe [...]. For if we are destroyed, the knowledge is dead, perhaps for good. We are model citizens, in our own special way; we walk the old tracks, we lie in the hills at night, and the city people let us be. We're stopped and searched occasionally, but there's nothing on our persons to incriminate us. The organization is flexible, very loose, and fragmentary. [...] [O]ver a period of twenty years or so, we met each other, travelling, and got the loose network together and set out a plan. [...] And when the war's over, some day, some year, the books can be written again, the people will be called in, one by one, to recite what they know [...]." (pp. 195–197)

Granger's explanations uncover a structural flaw that is inherent in most dystopias. His thinking reveals a fundamental evasiveness, there is no specific cultural or political vision that one would expect of dissidents. Significantly, the very absence of any socio-political statement makes the group seem naively idealistic and conservative. The dissident otherworld, then, stands for a return to the status quo ante, to a world that existed before "[t]he public itself stopped reading of its own accord" (p. 113), as Faber puts it. Thus an alternative political order created by the representatives of the dissidents is neither alluded to nor described in detail. It is the very nature of being a dissident that counts as the novel's motto by the Spanish poet Juan Ramón Jiménez (1881–1958) clearly shows: "If they give you ruled paper, write the other way."

Another aspect that deserves criticism refers to Granger's statement "the city people let us be." There is no rationale given why the rigid, conformist society that does not tolerate any form of non-conforming behaviour accepts the existence of the book people. In lieu of any other explanation it can only be argued that the plot demands such a group. Even though there is no programmatic vision the final outlook of the novel must not be seen as pessimistic. As each person stands for a different book, as each man memorizes a text he loves, the group, as fragmentary as it is, stands for radical cultural pluralism. And when Granger concludes his remarks with the following words: "Come on now, we're going to go build a mirror-factory first and put out nothing but mirrors for the next year and take a long look in them" (pp. 209 f), he voices his belief that post-holocaust man has to develop a new identity free from any political doctrines.

Fahrenheit 451 Today

The year 2003 saw the 50th anniversay of the novel's first publication date. To commemorate this event Simon & Schuster and Del Rey published special anniversary editions which, in turn, prompted some critics to reviews from the vantage point of 50 years of reading experience. Obviously, there are two different approaches. Critic Jeremy Smith writing for the online magazine *Strange Horizons* calls the novel a case of "Cassandraism" after the mythological figure Cassandra and comes up with the following verdict: "If the imaginative success of a Cassandraist novel as warning must be measured in direct proportion to its empirical failure as a prediction, then, at the beginning of the twenty-first century, *Fahrenheit 451* has devolved into a near-total fiasco." To support his judgement he quotes the author who in an interview in 1998 for the magazine *Wired* stated: "Almost everything in *Fahrenheit 451* has come about, one way or the other – the influence of television, the rise of local TV news, the neglect of education. As a result, one area of our society is brainless. But I utilized those things in the novel because I was trying to *prevent* a future, not *predict* one." Smith quite obviously reads the novel not as fiction but as a sociological study of the future, thereby ignoring a central premise of literature. It is neither the primary function of fiction to mirror reality nor its task to predict the future in an empirical way. Rather, the writer of fiction seeks to re-construct certain details of reality by giving them a new form, thus inviting the reader to see that portion of reality in a new and different light.

The *Wall Street Journal* critic John J. Miller, by contrast, praises Bradbury for exactly the opposite reasons: "Jules Verne is famous among science-fiction writers for predicting 20th century technologies, such as submarines and rocket ships. Mr Bradbury rivals him in *Fahrenheit 451*. He envisioned the popularity of headset radios, plus interactive TV and live new broadcasts." (J. J. Miller, "The Man Who Sounded The Fire Alarm – 'Fahrenheit 451', 50 Years Later", in: *The Wall Street Journal*, May 14, 2003, https://www.wjs.com/articles/SB105288055761123900) Miller then calls "this kind of prognostication remarkable" and the book "unforgettable". Similar to Smith, Miller also reduces a literary text to a sociological treatise thereby neglecting the literary dimension of the novel.

Of the anniversay reviews only critic Chris Przybyszewski writing for the online magazine *SF Site* does justice to the novel's literary texture by discussing elements of language, of plot and of characterization. On the whole his criticism is substantiated as in the following initial observation:

> "*Fahrenheit 451* is one of the more remarkable books of our time. Sure, the text has its share of warts. The characters are more like caricatures, over the top and thin in their complexity. Ray Bradbury indulges his inner high-school writer with his strong use of comparisons which, for example, describes the overhead sound of bombers as 'if two

> giant hands had torn ten thousand miles of black linen down the seam.' And I am not going to talk about descriptions, such as 'The subway fled past him, cream-tile, jet-black, cream-tile, jet-black, numerals and darkness, more darkness and the total adding itself.' Moreover, the ending is simplistic and idealistic, where the well read of society emerge from their homeless shelters to save a post-apocalyptic world." (www.sfsite.com/01b/fh192.htm)

Whatever we want to make of this, Przybyszewski is certainly right in observing that the "characters are [...] thin in their complexity" as they are basically representatives of ideas rather than individual characters. And we may also agree with his conclusion: The text offers no answers to the question posed. Instead, it offers a story about a man seeking truth.

The Film

Synopsis of the DVD Chapters

Chapter One [00.00 – 07.28] begins with an off-voice that informs us about the cast and the director of the film. At the same time the camera pans across various roofs and zooms in on different TV antennae. The background colour changes with each zoom-in.
We then see men dressed in black uniforms gliding down a pole and take up position on an old-fashioned, open fire engine. The camera follows the engine as it is driving towards its destination. In this part of the scene music is put to the film. There is a cut and the scene shifts to a medium shot of a man who is sitting at his breakfast table. An anonymous telephone caller warns him. The man hurriedly leaves his flat and the apartment block where he lives. At the same time the fire engine is arriving. The firemen enter the apartment and methodically search it for books. During their search music is heard again. Not one word is spoken. The books are found, collected and taken outside. A flame-thrower is handed to Montag who burns the books. Bystanders watch the burning as if it were nothing unusual.
The initial scene makes it clear that Montag has a leading role among the group of firemen, and it also reveals the fact that Montag is an absolute loyal fireman. Asked by Captain Beatty what he would do if mowing the lawn were forbidden he simply answers: "Watch it grow."
Chapter Two [07.29 – 13.23] starts with a shot of the monorail, a public transportation system. The camera captures some of the passengers' faces. We see a close-up of Montag's face which is devoid of any expression. The camera shifts to Clarisse's face which expresses liveliness and warmth. Clarisse approaches Montag and starts a conversation with him which is unusual as none of the passengers speak. Montag and Clarisse continue to talk for the rest of the time they spend together. Their conversation serves a didactic function, as the viewer learns something about the reason of the firemen's existence.
Chapter Three [13.25 – 19.25] is set inside Montag's house. Linda is watching TV on a large wall screen. She shows no interest in her husband; later we see her taking part in the "family" script, a soap where the actors ask a person named Linda to react to a question. Linda believes to be a genuine part of the script, whereas her husband makes her realize that some two hundred thousand Lindas across the country are spoken to in such a pre-fabricated way. – The first scene inside Montag's house shows the distance and indifference that exist between husband and wife. It also reveals that the roles of Linda and Clarisse are played by the same actress. Only the different hairstyle indicates that these roles belong to different persons.
In Chapter Four [19.27 – 26.32] there is a tracking shot of the fire engine as it is driven along a road and back to the station. The tracking shot is accompa-

Scene from François Truffaut's film *Fahrenheit 451* (1966) – © dpa Picture-Alliance (Everett Collection), Frankfurt/M.

nied by the background music. While the fire engine is being driven to its parking position the camera zooms in onto the heraldic symbol of the firemen, the phoenix, that is later to be seen on Captain Beatty's uniform as well. Inside the fire station Montag lectures a group of trainees on how to find hidden books. A loudspeaker requests him to go and see the Captain. At his office Captain Beatty speaks with Montag about his prospects for promotion. He signals his support.

Chapter Five [26.33 – 33.17] is again set at Montag's house. He returns home only to find his wife lying unconsciously on the floor. Montag calls the emergency service and is put through to "Poison". Paramedics arrive and treat Linda's suicide attempt as an everyday matter. The next morning Linda remembers nothing. However, she feels refreshed and seduces Montag.

Chapter Six [33.18 – 39.26] is made up of a series of cuts. We see Montag inside the monorail, we see his wife watching TV, and Montag returning from work. He hides a book in a cabinet in the bathroom, thus committing his first breach of law. Late at night he gets up and starts to read the book. The lines are shown in a close-up and we can follow Montag's slow reading. Then there is a flashback to a scene on a playground. The firemen are searching people's belongings for books. Captain Beatty takes a tiny book from an infant. There is a medium shot of Beatty, the phoenix symbol is clearly visible on his helmet and on his outfit. With this scene the role of firemen as a kind of secret police or Gestapo is clearly established.

Chapter Seven [39.27 – 46.08] begins with Montag leaving his house and going to the monorail station. He is followed by Clarisse and an older woman. Inside the monorail Clarisse watches Montag. The point of view makes it clear that Montag doesn't see her. After Montag gets off Clarisse hurries off, too. There are tracking shots of her running to a bridge where she 'accidentally' bumps into Montag. They go to a café which is opposite the entrance of the fire station. Close-ups of Clarisse's face reveal her agitated and flustered state of mind. Montag learns that she has been dismissed from her teaching job. While they are talking the camera pans to a man outside who is about to throw something into the information box. Clarisse calls him an informer, Montag corrects her and points out that he is an informant. Clarisse persuades him to go to her school with her; she phones Captain Beatty, pretends to be Linda Montag and says that Montag has been taken ill.

Chapter Eight [46.10 – 49.31] is shot inside the school. Clarisse and Montag are walking down a corridor. A boy comes towards her, then turns around abruptly and hurries back into his classroom. The act is repeated by another boy. Clarisse's belongings are thrown around a corner, the bag is gliding on the floor towards her. The scene makes it clear that Clarisse is treated like a pariah. Inside the school's elevator Montag consoles the crying Clarisse. He looks tense and concentrated, at the same time his face expresses concern and compassion.

When he confesses to her that he has started reading a book he is filmed from a slight bird's eye view as if to underline his new vulnerability.
Chapter Nine [49.33 – 52.26] is set again at Montag's house. Linda wakes up at night to find her husband reading. She also discovers the hidden books in the bathroom's cabinet. She calls the books "things", he refers to them as his "family". A quarrel ensues, Montag sends Linda back to bed and continues his reading. The next morning he goes to work, inside the fire station he cannot glide up the pole anymore and has to take the stairs.
Chapter Ten [52.28 – 1.03.54] marks the turning point in the action. It begins with an alarm, there are close-ups of the red siren, a red phoenix, the number 551 in red and there is an excessive use of red as background colour, all of which prepare the ground for the dramatic impact of the action to follow. Tracking shots accompany the fire engine on its way to its destination which turns out to be an old house with a secret library. Inside the firemen are filmed from above as if taking up position; the sole occupant of the house, an old lady, is filmed from a low angle. The respective angles are of symbolic significance, they indicate that the woman is beyond reach. She cannot be threatened or intimidated; the firemen, by contrast, are insignificant, they do not know anything about culture, heritage or man's traditions. After the secret library has been discovered Beatty takes Montag on a tour. He lectures him on the necessity of burning books, on the egalitarian philosophy of the state and on the need for eliminating everything that is non-conformist. Close-ups of their faces reveal Montag's shock and Beatty's triumphant state of mind.
Montag secretly picks up a book and puts it into his bag. He is watched by another fireman who sees what Montag is doing. – The firemen prepare the burning of both the house and the books. Their preparations are accompanied by music. The camera captures the blue liquid that is being sprayed on the books. Numerous book titles are shown in close-ups, the titles indicate that the books are from all areas of fiction and science. Thus mankind's cultural heritage is here symbolically destroyed. The woman refuses to leave the house. She ignites the fire by a lighting a match. A series of medium shots show how the flames devour everything.
Chapter 11 [1.03.56 – 1.10.06] stands in marked contrast to the previous action. There is a ladies' party at Linda's. Montag returns from his action and immediately goes into the bedroom to hide another book. He is totally uncommunicative. He then enters the living-room, turns off the TV wall and forces Linda's friends to listen to his reading. Their faces reveal sheer incomprehension and incredulity while listening to Montag's recitals. One lady even starts to cry. The content of his reading is called "filth", his behaviour "cruel".
Chapter 12 [1.10.08 – 1.21.40] is also set at Montag's house. The couple is sleeping; Montag is having a bad dream about the previous day; Clarisse is replaced by the old woman at the house and it is she who ignites the fire and sinks down to be burned.

A siren wakes Clarisse up. The firemen are outside. A frightened Clarisse climbs onto the roof. The following morning Montag looks feverish. Linda insists on Montag's taking away the books, else she will leave him. Outside, Montag sees the barricaded house in which Clarisse and her uncle used to live. A neighbour informs him that they have been taken away. – Montag returns to the fire station. He breaks into the locked office of the Captain and frantically looks for something, obviously information on the whereabouts of Clarisse. When a surprised Beatty comes back into his office he shows Montag the list of last night's arrests.
When Montag learns that Clarisse is still at large, he collapses onto the floor. Shakily he leaves the fire station. There is a cut to his house. Linda is leaving the house. She drops Montag's photo into the info box at the fire station, thus letting the firemen know that he has books. A medium shot of her face conveys relief and, at the same time, a brief sadness.
Chapter 13 [1.21.41 – 1.27.51] begins with a long shot of the approaching monorail. Clarisse walks down the ladder. Montag who has waited behind a pillar for her, goes with her to her former house. Together they look for a list of dissidents that her uncle has kept. Montag finds it and burns it. Clarisse confesses to Montag that their first encounter was not accidental. She informs him about the existence of "the book people", their location and gives him directions how to get there. She urges Montag to come with her, but he prefers to stay and to work against the system by planting books in every fireman's house. There is a cut to Montag's house where Linda is packing a suitcase.
Chapter 14 [1.27.53 – 1.34.20] marks the climax of the action. At the fire station the firemen get ready for a mission. Montag tells Beatty that he is leaving the force. Betty does not accept his resignation at this point and makes him come along. There are tracking shots of the fire engine as it is driven across the countryside. The tracking shots are accompanied by music. A detail shot of the phoenix symbol at the front of the car once again brings the destructive nature of the firemen's work sharply into focus. When the fire engine arrives at Montag's house, Linda is stepping outside, carrying a suitcase. Her farewell words – "I couldn't bear it anymore" – refer to Montag's having started to read books. Inside the house Montag is told to collect the books he has hidden. He is given the sparkler and told to burn them. Instead, he turns on the sparkler so that it becomes a flame-thrower and burns his bedroom. Then he turns it on the books. There are various close-ups of the books as they are being devoured by the flames. In slow motion the pages dissolve and are burnt to ashes. The whole process is accompanied by music; there is also a detail shot of the text of a page and how it is slowly eaten up by the fire. When Beatty tries to take a book that Montag has hidden inside his uniform by force Montag threatens him with a gun and turns the flame-thrower on him. Pointing the flame-thrower at the other firemen he manages to drive them away.

Chapter 15 [1.34.22 – 1.37.37] centres around Montag's escape. He is shown running across a field. There is a cut to a red car with a loudspeaker. Its speaker calls on the people to look out for Montag who is "wanted for murder". Montag makes it to the river and hides under the tarpaulin in a boat. There are four flying airmen who are looking out for him and do not detect him. Montag paddles across the river and is seen walking along the railroad tracks. Medium shots of his face show his agitation and anticipation.
Chapter 16 [1.37.39 – 1.47.32] is set in the woods where the "book people" live. Montag is welcomed and watches his own faked death in front of the fire station on TV. The leader of the group who refers to themselves as "a minority of undesirables" explains their activities to Montag. Each person memorizes a book that is then destroyed. Montag opts for memorizing Poe's *Tales of Mystery and Imagination*. There are various shots of the idyllic countryside with people walking about, reciting their books. Montag and Clarisse are walking together, and Montag is reading from his book whose text he tries to memorize. Unlike the novel the film does not end on a note of hope. The last scene presents a winter landscape with the book people walking up and down at a lakeside reciting the books they have memorized.

Comparison of Book and Film

When comparing François Truffaut's film *Fahrenheit 451* (1966) to the novel one immediately notices three major differences that concern the list of persons. To begin with, the roles of Mildred (called Linda in the film) and Clarisse are played by the same actress, Julie Christie. Secondly, Faber is absent in the film. Thirdly, Clarisse survives and functions as Montag's guide to the book people, thus replacing Faber. Other differences refer to the fact that the atomic war which annihilates the city is not mentioned at the end of the film; furthermore, there is no Mechanical Hound.
Apart from these obvious changes there are important minor differences between the script of the film and the text of the novel. For instance, the following dialogue between Clarisse and Montag is not to be found in the novel but helps to explain why the film director has made the casting decision mentioned above:

> I don't think I've seen your wife. What's she like?
> She's rather like you, except her hair is long.
> Rather like me?
> Quite like you.

Contrary to the novel the scenes in the TV parlour are presented extensively and the dialogues spoken in the soaps are revealed in their total banality. Here Truffaut quite obviously wanted to draw the attention to the emptiness and meaninglessness of the TV programmes.

In contrast to the novel Clarisse is a teacher on probation and an active member of a dissident group. As she confesses to Montag: "I always wanted to tell you our meeting in the monorail [i.e. skytrain] was no accident. I noticed you and I followed you. I thought you could help us." She urges him to come with her to the book people, but Montag isn't ready yet, saying: "I must stay in the city. I have a plan. I will hide a book in every firemen's house and then denounce him. The system will eat itself." Montag's initiative, his can-do attitude at this point of the film contrasts strikingly with the haltingness of the novel's protagonist who needed guidance and support from Faber. In the film, however, there seem to be two Montags present from early on.
After Montag has arrived at the site of the book people he is given the following rationale for their existence:

> "We are a minority of undesirables crying out in the wilderness. But it won't always be so. One day we shall be called on, one by one, to recite what we have learned. And then books will be printed again. And when the next age of darkness comes, those who come after us will do again as we have done."

Set against the words spoken by Granger in the novel this explanation is vague to the point of meaninglessness. One is left wondering what is meant by "age of darkness", and one cannot help feeling that the director and his script writer tried to circumvent any grappling with the novel's open ending. Significantly, the religious overtones that are apparent in the novel, for example in Montag's memorizing *The Revelations of St. John* and in his quoting from it at the very end (cf. p. 211) are not to be found in the film. Here Montag memorizes the *Tales of Mystery and Imagination* by Edgar Allan Poe, thus undercutting the note of optimism and hope inherent in the final quote from *The Revelations*.

Analysis of Selected Scenes

Before the actual narration of the film begins there is a title sequence composed of quick shots which zoom in on TV antennas, each shot tinted a different colour. The credits are not written but spoken, each name or set of names corresponding to one shot in the montage. The significance of this peculiar avoidance of written names will emerge soon: the society depicted in the film has completely forbidden any form of written communication.
After the credits the first narrative sequence starts, which involves the firemen who are called on duty. Throughout the film, the firemen's raids will be portrayed through brief, roughly edited shots, utilizing many close-ups. Panning and tracking are rare. The firemen's musical theme, which is also introduced at this point, is played staccato and has an intense rhythm.
In contrast to this exposition the film's next narrative segment is constructed quite differently. This sequence takes place in the apartment of a book

reader and begins with a long take following the person through his apartment from room to room. There is no incidental music, which creates an eerie atmosphere throughout the whole scene. – The first DVD chapter also introduces the fireman Montag at the raid. Medium shots emphasize the efficiency with which he works. Chapters 3 and 5 introduce Montag's wife Linda (as she is called in the film) and focus on Montag's special cinematic role. In chapter 3 the continual use of crosscutting (i.e. the alternation of shots in a scene) involving the couple's conversation underlines the alienation between the partners. As this conversation starts immediately after that with Clarisse, a strong opposition is revealed. On the whole, crosscutting in *Fahrenheit 451* tends to suggest opposition, separation and conflict, e.g. in the following scene: After performing in the "family theatre" Linda asks Montag: "Don't you think I should have been an actress?" His response, in the next shot, is given after a gap of several hours. Montag is shown in bed, and says, "What?" Then the camera cuts to Linda, also in bed, who repeats, "I said, don't you think I should have been an actress?" Montag finally replies, "Oh, yes ... yes ... ."

Throughout the film Montag is drawn in two directions, torn between his life as a fireman and his interest in non-conformists like Clarisse. This aspect is reflected in the double role of Julie Christie as Linda and as Clarisse. "Two" Montags correspond to both women: one is a loyal and committed fireman and husband and the other one reads books, and kills his captain in the end. At one point this doubling occurs in one single scene. Montag returns home to find his wife unconscious from an overdose of sleeping pills. He is shown going around the house, and the camera follows him from room to room, telephone to telephone, pill-bottle to pill-bottle. The paramedics arrive and Montag sits down to wait for them to finish. While he is waiting, a close-up of his face is superimposed on the end of the previous shot; this doubling lasts much longer than a normal dissolve marking a lapse of time. The "two" Montags thus remain on the screen until an off-voice says: "You can come in now, sir." Then the former shot fades and there remains only "one" Montag who goes in to his wife.

A further interesting segment concerns Montag's first reading (cf. DVD chapter 6). The passage he reads from Dickens' *David Copperfield* deals with being born, which is a parallel to Montag who is indeed reborn through the process of reading the book. He sits with his back to the blank television wall screen and reads aloud by its light. In a quick series of shots we see first the book page with Montag's finger following the words, then cutting closer again and again until only one word at a time is seen, the camera panning to follow the text at the rate of Montag's reading. When he comes to the end of a line, the camera pans all the way back to the beginning of the next line and starts again. It does not show all the words simultaneously but has been reduced to capture the linear, letter-by-letter approach of Montag's reading, thus empha-

sizing the frustratingly slow pace of his hesitant reading as well as the fact that in this society people are kept in a state of semi-illiteracy.
The last two units (Montag's arrival in the woods and the long final shot marking the end of the film; see DVD chapter 16) correspond to the first two segments of the film (the credits and the initial presentation of the firemen). Truffaut's film ends with a long, slow zoom-out shot of the camp in the woods, in which the book people walk around a lake reciting the books they have identified with. Their voices, mingled on the soundtrack, grow fainter as a slow music dominates. This shot is a clear reference to the film's beginning. The zoom-ins of the title segment are opposed to the single, long zoom-out of the end; the one off-voice has been replaced by a multitude of individual voices, thus capturing the fundamental development the film depicts: from a uniformed, conformist fireman to a member of the multi-voiced book people.

The Reception of the Film: A Review and its Analysis

Bosley Crowther, "Screen: 'Fahrenheit 451' Makes Burning Issue Dull; Truffaut's First Film in English Opens Plaza Picture Presents Dual Julie Christie", in: The New York Times, November 15, 1966; https://ny.times.com/1966/11/15/archives/screen-fahrenheit-451-makes-burning-issue-dull-truffauts-first-film.html

If François Truffaut were trying to make literature seem dull and the whole hideous practice of book-burning seem no more shocking than putting a blow-torch to a pile of leaves, he could not have accomplished his purpose much better than he unintentionally has in his first motion picture made in English, "Fahrenheit 451."
Holy smoke! What a pretentious and pedantic production he has made of Ray Bradbury's futuristic story of a fireman in a hypothetical state where all reading matter is forbidden and the fire department's job is to police the citizens who try to keep books in hiding! It burns books instead of putting out fires.
And, furthermore, what a dismal fellow Oskar Werner manages to make this solemnly regimented fireman who finally gets a hankering for books and becomes a fire-department dropout when he falls for a schoolteacher who owns a secret copy of the Memoirs of Saint-Simon.
I can only suggest to you how dismal and unexciting he is - and by this demonstration show you how bloodless and pompous is the film - by telling you that the schoolteacher for whom he conceives a high regard is a bleakly defeminized version of his elegant, sexy wife who doesn't care beans for reading and gets all her information from watching the wall-to-wall television screen.
Now, I do not suggest for one moment that the idea elucidated here is not fundamentally wholesome. A woman who bravely reads books is more likely to be socially constructive than one who is hung on TV. And the contrast arranged by Mr. Truffaut - a homely bookworm versus a beauteous TV fan - is a suitable one for illustrating the austerity of dedication to books.
But it makes for pretty dreary entertainment when you have to sit there and watch a frozen-faced Mr. Werner piously turn away from a long-haired, voluptuous Julie Christie

> and go marching off down the railway tracks in quest of the bleak, bobbed-haired Miss Christie who has gone to the land where the book-people are.
> And it also makes you wonder just how sound Mr. Truffaut is in his labored enthusiasm for the glories of literature when he shows us the method of preserving the great books in his benighted state. It is by having people commit them to memory and go around reciting them by rote.
> Nothing could be more depressing than seeing people ambling through the woods of what looks to be a sort of adult literary camp, mechanically reciting "The Pickwick Papers" and Plato's "Dialogues," or seeing a dying man compelling his grandson to recite after him and commit to memory Robert Louis Stevenson's unfinished "Weir of Hermiston." What a dismal image we have here of the deathless eloquence of literature!
> Now, of course, it could be that Mr. Truffaut is really trying to pull our legs in this seeming allegorical polemic, which came to the Plaza yesterday. It could be that he is trying, to tease us with a deadpan travesty of an attitude of social indignation, which is actually somewhat threadbare, after all. Mr. Bradbury's novel came out in 1953, and we all had known the shock and outrage of book-burning long before that.
> But it's hard to believe that Mr. Truffaut could be guilty of such poor taste. Poor writing, yes, and dull direction, but certainly not poor taste! He wouldn't dare put into a picture intended to be a joke a scene so ugly and currently evocative as one of a captured book-lover setting herself afire.
> Nor would he allow a subtle put-on to be so ponderous and humorless.
> No, it strikes me that Mr. Truffaut simply got himself tangled up with an idea that called for slashing satire of a sort beyond his grasp, and with language he couldn't fashion into lively and witty dialogue. The consequence is a dull picture - dully fashioned and dully played - which is rendered all the more sullen by the dazzling color in which it is photographed.
> The title, incidentally, means the heat at which paper ignites. There's no need to worry for a moment about the combustion point of film.

Analysis

New York Times critic Bosley Crowther has written a devastating critique or slating. There is not one aspect of the film that he likes. The opening paragraph of his review immediately sets the tone: in a condescending way the writer makes fun of French director François Truffaut by implying that his directing was so poor that it made "literature seem dull" and the burning of books a petty affair. The initial observation is carried into the second paragraph. An exclamation, an inversion ("what [...] he has made"), which underlines his negative opinion, and the use of negative adjectives ("pretentious", "pedantic") that are highlighted by the alliteration make it clear that Crowther intensely dislikes the film. In the third paragraph he presents the first example from the film. He calls Oskar Werner's performance "dismal" and then goes on to note that the whole film is "bloodless and pompous." This value judgement is introduced by a direct address to the reader: "I can only suggest to you," thereby making the reader an accomplice of his own line of thinking.

Scene from Truffaut's *Fahrenheit 451* with Julie Christie and Oskar Werner.

Next the critic discusses the dual role of Julie Christie which he finds fault with. According to him, Clarisse is but “a bleakly defeminized version of [Montag's] elegant, sexy wife”. He calls Oskar Werner's search for Clarisse “pretty dreary entertainment” insinuating that no one would leave “a sexy wife” for “the bleak, bobbed-haired” Clarisse. It will have become obvious by now that the reviewer mainly works with value judgements and assertions which he does not support by arguments or by presenting evidence from the film. This holds all the more true when one takes a closer look at his discussion of the book people. Here the reviewer states: “Nothing could be more depressing than seeing people ambling through the woods of what looks to be a sort of adult literary camp mechanically reciting [...].” It remains unclear why this scene is “depressing” and his exclamation “What a dismal image we have here of the deathless eloquence of literature” is nothing but an unfounded stipulation that is nowhere backed up by arguments.
The criticism becomes even more scathing in the paragraphs to follow. Crowther pretends to feel sympathy with the French director by alleging the following: “It could be that he is trying to tease us with a deadpan travesty or an attitude of social indignation.” However, as Crowther immediately qualifies his sympathy by observing “it's hard to believe that Truffaut could be guilty of such poor taste” this shows once again his condescending attitude. Crowther then concludes that Truffaut was not up to the challenge the plot poses, that it was “beyond his grasp”. The final blow “a dull picture – dully fashioned and dully played”– together with the final pun “there is no need to worry about the combustion point of film” highlight a review in which the writer shows little understanding of the film, much less of the novel. The review thus has to be qualified as one-sided and polemical as the writer nowhere seeks to support his negative view by arguments.

The Intertextuality of *Fahrenheit 451*

Fahrenheit 451, Bradbury's fifth book and first true novel, evolved from the 1951 *Galaxy Science Fiction Magazine* novella "The Fireman" and from a number of short stories such as "The Exiles" (1949), "Usher II" (1950) or "The Smile" (1952). As regards "The Fireman", Bradbury followed in *Fahrenheit 451* the same basic plot sequences. Many brief references in the novella became full scenes in the novel, notably the lengthy talks between Montag and Beatty and Montag and Faber. Thus characters were fleshed-out and expanded, and the symbolism was added to the novel. Significantly, the character of Montag's wife was also greatly deepened. In the novel she and Clarisse are presented as antithetical figures.

There are a few changes, however, that deserve closer study. Whilst in the novel Beatty provokes his own death – "Go ahead now, you second-hand litterateur, pull the trigger" (p. 154) – the Montag of "The Fireman" clearly intents to kill his superior who is called Leahy in the novella: "Montag was stunned by the thought of murder, for murder is always a new thing, and Montag knew nothing of murder; he knew only burning and burning things that people said were evil. 'I know what's really wrong with the world,' said Montag. 'Look here, Montag,' cried Leahy. And then he was a shrieking blaze, a jumping, sprawling, gibberish thing." (Nolan/Greenberg, eds., 1980, p. 50)

Not surprisingly, the novella's ending also differs markedly from the novel. Montag does not carry *The Book of Ecclesiastes* in his head but *The Book of Job* which depicts Job's suffering and his futile attempts at finding an answer to the question why God has punished him even though he led a god-fearing life. In the novella there is no reference to the mythical Phoenix and to the final quote taken from *The Book of Revelations* (cf. 2:7; 22:2; 22:19) which refers to the re-gaining of paradise. The optimistic note on which the novel closes is absent in "The Fireman". Here Montag first quotes from *Ecclesiates* 3:2 – "To everything there is a season, and a time to every purpose under the heaven [...]" – and then from *The Book of Job*: "Man that is born of a woman is of few days and full of trouble." Particularly the last quote which emphasizes the nature of affliction inherent in man's life provides the novella's ending with a grim and pessimistic outlook.

Apart from these changes there were two incidents that prompted Bradbury to expand his earlier version. One of these incidents refers to a personal recollection of a fire at his grandmother's house: "There, climbing the wall, was a bright monster [...] it made a great oven-roaring sound [...] as it ate the wallpaper and devoured the ceiling [...] I never forgot it. Perhaps it was all these memories [...] of the fiendish fire itself that caused 'Fahrenheit 451' to grow – from notes to paragraph to story to novel." (Quoted after: Nolan, "Editor's Afterword", 1980, p. 72) The other incident that stimulated him to expand the novella into the novel-length version was the attempt at library censorship imposed by the infamous Senator McCarthy. Bradbury was greatly disturbed at the idea of being told which books he could or could not read. "So I wrote about a totalitarian," he says. "A stupid man, a prejudiced man who in the midst of this nightmare wakes himself up and begins to look around and realize he's burning the ideals of the world." (ibid.)

As for the stories that preceded "The Fireman" as well as *Fahrenheit 451* "The Exiles" is clearly the most important forerunner. Set in the year 2120 inside a space ship and on Mars "The Exiles" has at its narrative centre two ideas that were to be put to use again in *Fahrenheit 451*. On board are two hundred books, the last remaining copies of such fiction as *Tales of Mystery and Imagination* by Edgar Allan Poe, *Frankenstein* by Mary Shelley or *Alice in Wonderland* by Lewis Carroll, all of which "were destroyed a century ago. By law" ("The Exiles", p. 96). The space ship's captain has taken the last remaining copies from locked museum vaults along because he intends to burn them on Mars once they have arrived there. This decision is based on mysterious dreams members of the crew had prior to their start from earth. Their dreams resembled witchcraft-induced nightmares in which men were bitten by white rats who drank their blood or had become a white wolf that was shot and buried with a stake in his heart. The action on board the space ship is paralleled by a strand of action set on Mars. The planet is populated by spiritual creatures from the world of magic, imagination and witchcraft who incorporate authors and literary figures from books forbidden long ago on earth. Realizing that the space ship is about to land in an hour these creatures are determined to fight off the Earthmen:

> "They won't be prepared for us, at least. They haven't the imagination. Those clean young rocket men with their antiseptic bloomers and fish-bowl helmets, with their new religion. About their necks, on gold chains, scalpels. Upon their heads, a diadem of miroscopes. In their holy fingers, steaming incense urns which in reality are only germicidal ovens for steaming out superstition. The names of Poe, Bierce, Hawthorne, Blackwood – blasphemy to their clean lips." (ibid., p. 99)

This passage makes it clear that a clash of different cultures is about to occur. The world of imagination and magic as represented by books that were destroyed and the world of reason and science are at loggerheads. In the words of Edgar Allan Poe, one of the people living on Mars:

> "On Earth, a century ago, in the year 2020 they outlawed our books. [...] I only know that our worlds and our creations called us and we tried to save them, and the only saving thing we could do was wait out the century here on Mars, hoping Earth might overweight itself with these scientists and their doubtings; but now they are coming to clean us out of here, us and our dark things, and all the alchemists, witches, vampires, and were things that, one by one, retreated across space as science made inroads through every country on Earth and finally left no alternative at all but exodus." (ibid., p. 101)

However, the creatures on Mars are doomed, as one character puts it bluntly:

> "'What happens to us on the day that when the *last* copies of our books are destroyed? [...] Death! *Real* death for all of us. We exist only through Earth's sufferance. If a final edict tonight destroyed our last few words we'd be like lights put out.'
> And this is exactly what happens. After the space ship has landed the captain orders the books taken along to be burnt: 'The old world left behind. A new start. What more symbolic than that we here dedicate ourselves all the more firmly to science and progress. [...] A new world. With a gesture we burn the last of the old.'" (ibid., p. 105)

These words later echoed by Captain Beatty reveal that science and imagination, progress and the realm of the subconscious are considered to be detrimental, if not antithetical forces and therefore have to be suppressed – hence the censorship of books on earth, hence the burning of the last copies on Mars.
"Usher II", which is part of *The Martian Chronicles*, is set on Mars. The year is 2005, a character named William Stendahl has a House of Usher built in the memory of Edgar Allan Poe whose writings together with those of other gothic novelists were burned on earth. Stendahl's explanation is almost literally repeated later by Captain Beatty:

> "Oh, it started very small. In 1950 and '60 it was a grain of sand. They began by controlling books of cartoons and then detective books and, of course, films, one way or another, one group or another, political bias, religious prejudice, union pressures; there was always a minority afraid of something, and a great majority afraid of the dark, afraid of the future, afraid of the past, afraid of the present, afraid of themselves and shadows of themselves." ("Usher II", p. 105)

Similar to *Fahrenheit 451* there is a special organization called "Moral Climate people" who see to it that even on Mars no deviations from terrestric laws are tolerated. Hence a special team called "The Dismantlers and Burning Crew" looks after deviants and destroys any artefacts. Unlike Montag, however, the main character of "Usher II" manages to outwit the Officer from Moral Climate and has him killed. The appeal of the story lies in Bradbury's ability to have his main character turn the technological gadgets against their own inventors by creating robotic clones of enemy characters and have these clones kill the original person.
The idea of destroying and burning books is also taken up in the story "The Smile". The story is set in a barren post-apocalyptic United States in the future, in which cultural values have been profoundly inverted. The future society is held together by ritualized Roman circuslike ceremonies in which people burn and mutilate books and other cultural artefacts:

> "And Tom thought of the festivals in the past few years. The year they tore up all the books in the square and burned them and everyone was drunk and laughing. And the festival of science a month ago when they dragged in the last motorcar and picked lots and each lucky man who won was allowed one smash of a sledge hammer at the car." ("The Smile", p. 112)

In the present instance the people are lining up early in the morning for "the day of the festival" to spit on the Mona Lisa. A young boy Tom, the main character of the short story, is wondering why they are all there in line to spit (cf. p. 111). A grown-up by the name of Grigsby explains to him (and thus to the reader) the following:

> "'Well Tom, there's lots of reason. […] It has to do with hate. Hate for everything in the Past. I ask you, Tom, how did we get in such a state, cities all junk, roads like jigsaws from bombs, and half the cornfields glowing with radio-activity at night? Ain't that a lousy stew, I ask you?'
> 'Yes, sir, I guess so.'
> 'It's this way, Tom. You hate whatever it was that got you knocked down and ruined. That's human nature. Unthinking, maybe, but human nature anyway.'
> 'There's hardly nobody or nothing we don't hate,' said Tom.
> 'Right! The whole blooming kaboodle of them people in the Past who run the world.'" (p. 112)

Highbrow cultural artefacts then have become the centre and focus of the people's hatred for their one time elite. All remnants of their former civilization are destroyed, just as the Mona Lisa after it has been spat on is given over to the people: "The crowd was in full cry, their hands like so many hungry birds pecking away at the portrait." (p. 114) Tom manages to secure a piece of the painting's canvas which, as it turns out, is the Smile. The thematic link with *Fahrenheit 451*, then, is threefold. First, there is the inversion of cultural values; artefacts of mankind's cultural heritage are destroyed for pleasure rather than kept; secondly, an atomic war has devasted the country to a large extent; thirdly, both Tom, who seeks to preserve part of a cultural artefact, and Grigsby, who argues for the annihilation of culture, are forerunners of Montag and Captain Beatty.

3 Fast Facts

Outline 1: Structure and Development of the Plot

Outline 2: Montag's Development from State Guardian to Rebel

Outline 3: A Summary of Beatty's Lecture

Outline 4: Faber's Philosophy

Outline 5: Relationships between the Central Characters

Outline 6: Outline 6: The Bi-partite Structure of *Fahrenheit 451*

Outline 1: Structure and Development of the Plot

Part One: The Hearth and the Salamander

- Introduction of Montag, Clarisse, Mildred and Captain Beatty
- Beginning change of Montag: doubts set in
- Contrasts between Mildred and Clarisse established
- Burning of the heretic old woman and her books
- Beatty's defense of the dystopian state and its philosophy

Part Two: The Sieve and the Sand

- Montag's violation of norms: reading of books
- Montag's alliance with Faber
- Montag's increasing illegal activities: poetry reading
- Failure of communication between Montag and Mildred
- Firemen at Montag's house

Part Three: Burning Bright

- Montag burns his house and kills the Captain.
- He escapes into the wilderness outside the city.
- He meets the book people.
- He witnesses the destruction of the city.

Outline 2: Montag's Development from State Guardian to Rebel

- Conversation with Clarisse.

  Doubts set in; Montag begins to ask himself if he is happy.

- Mildred's suicide; blood transfusion.

  Montag displays a new thoughtfulness.

- Threatening gesture by the Mechanical Hound confirms Montag's feeling of being different.

  Conversation with Clarisse.

  For the first time Montag perceives with all his senses the smell and taste of Nature.

- Disappearance of Clarisse.

  Montag starts to think about his past.

  Alleged death of Clarisse.

  Montag experiences a severe emotional crisis; he confesses to Mildred his possession of books.

- Captain Beatty's lecture.

  Montag starts to have serious doubts about his job; he tries to read a book together with Mildred.

  Conversation with Faber.

  Montag develops subversive thoughts against the firemen.

- TV parlour party.

  Montag admits to having books and reads poetry to Mildred's friends.

- Killing of Beatty and destruction of the Mechanical Hound.

  Montag becomes an overt rebel.

- Montag's arrival at the bonfire of the book people.

  He joins the group of dissidents.

Outline 3: A Summary of Beatty's Lecture

Train of thought / major stylistyic devices / function

- history of firemen's profession
- rhetorial questions; enumeration
- to elicit consens; to impress the listener

- trend towards mass exploitation; examples of mass exploitation
- enumeration; antithetical contrast ("roomy" vs. "full"); metaphors ("paste pudding norm", "centrifuge")
- to stress the differences between the past and the present; to stress the idea of uniformity and the elimination of thought

- idea of political correctness and conformity
- series of enumeration; short declarative sentences; staccato style
- to hammer information into Montag; to avoid having to argue

- egalitarian philosophy; role of firemen
- use of imperatives; euphemism, contrast ("custodians of peace" vs. "dread of being inferior")
- to emphasize the special role of the firemen

- happiness as the central aim of life vs. books as troublemakers
- short sentences, exclamations, imperatives
- to underline Beatty's depiction of the state's social philosophy

- re-evaluation of fire as cleansing
- reversal
- to stress the function of fire as a force that stabilizes happiness

- information about the McClellans
- use of slandering words ("antisocial", "time bomb", "queer")
- to emphasize the need for happiness; to appeal to the listener's consent

- depiction of various forms of mass entertainment
- series of enumerations; uses of imperatives
- to emphasize the need for happiness; to appeal to the listener's consent

- summarizing description of the role of firemen
- use of flood imagery ("tide", "dike", "torrent"); use of inclusive "we", of anaphora and of imperatives
- to stress the vital role of firemen as society's safeguards; to strengthen the in-group feeling; to appeal to Montag's professional ethos

Outline 4: Faber's Philosophy

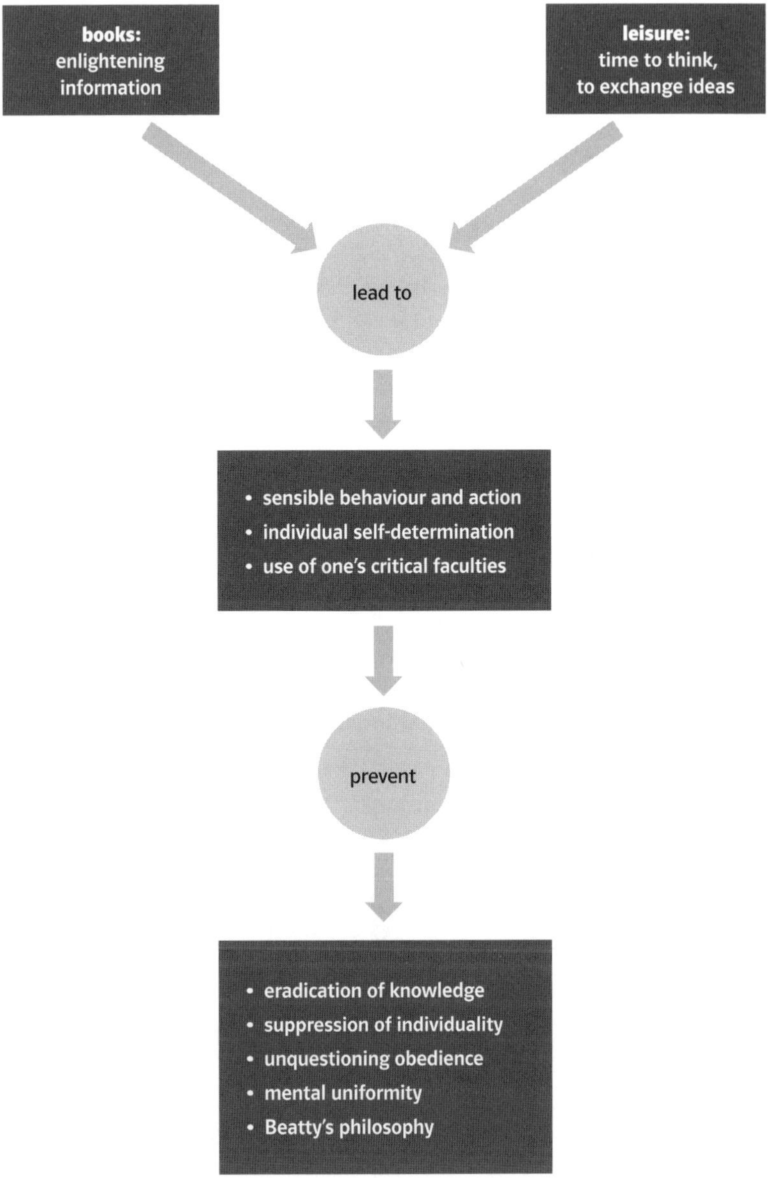

Outline 5: Relationships between the Central Characters

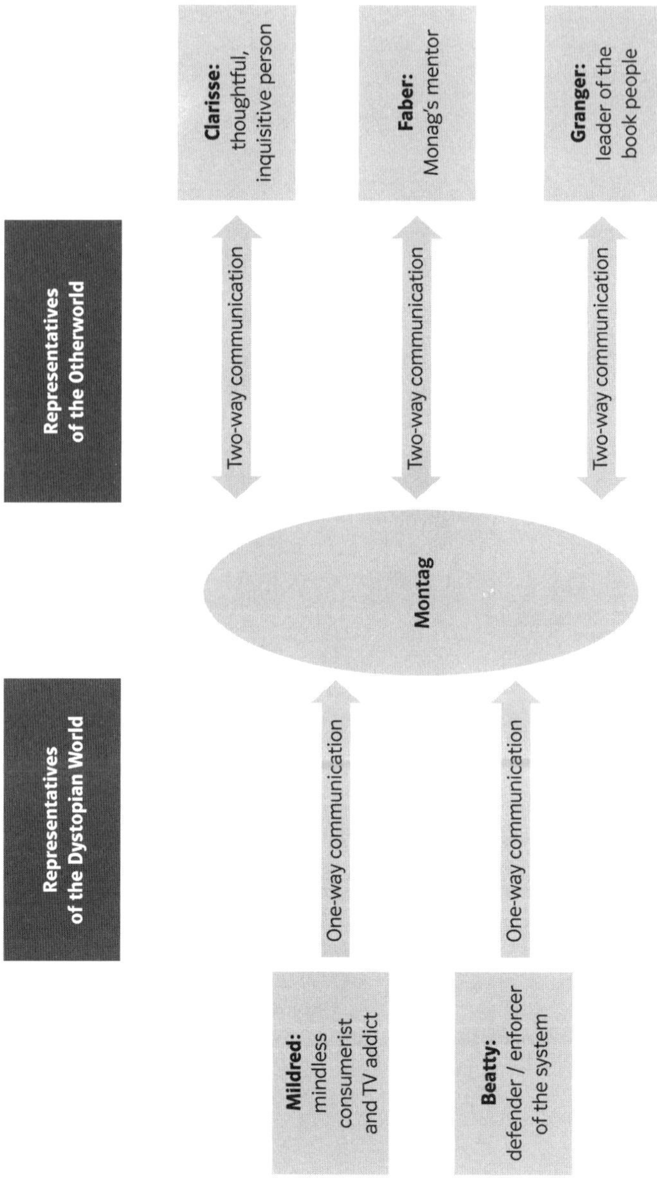

Outline 6: The Bi-partite Structure of *Fahrenheit 451*

Dystopian Society

- city
- permanent state of war
- banning and burning of books
- Mechanical Hound
- TV consumerism, theme parks
- state-induced mindless happiness
- "Life is immediate" – no history, no past
- conformity, no deviation from the norm

Function: to criticize aspects of contemporary society by extrapolating them into the future

Reversal

World of the Book People

- country, wilderness
- unspoiled nature
- living books
- absence of terror instruments
- simple life, silence
- contemplation
- preservation of man's cultural history
- non-conformity; self-determined individuals; dissidents

Function: to present an alternative to the mainstream society

4 Model Questions and Tasks

1. Content-related Questions
2. Interpreting Different Aspects of the Novel
3. Truffaut's Film
4. Creative Writing

1. Content-related Questions

1.1 Part One of the Novel

1.1.1 Who are the firemen and what do they do for a living?
1.1.2 What does Montag think of his job when he is introduced at the beginning?
1.1.3 What do we learn about Clarisse during her first meeting with Montag?
1.1.4 Why does Mildred need help when Montag gets home?
1.1.5 Describe the help that she receives. What is unusual about it?
1.1.6 How does Mildred react when she wakes up the following morning?
1.1.7 What does Mildred do all day?
1.1.8 In what respects is Clarisse different from Mildred?
1.1.9 What is the Mechanical Hound and what is its purpose?
1.1.10 What is the Hound's reaction to Montag? In what way is this significant?
1.1.11 Why does society consider Clarisse "anti-social"?
1.1.12 Who is Mildred's family?
1.1.13 What has happened to Clarisse? How did it happen?
1.1.14 List three different aspects Beatty lectures Montag about.

1.2 Part Two of the Novel

1.2.1 Who is Faber? Why is he reluctant to talk to Montag on the phone?
1.2.2 Why is Faber so critical of himself and pessimistic about the world when he is first introduced? Why is he then willing to help Montag?
1.2.3 What is Montag given before he leaves Faber's house?
1.2.4 Why are the characters on the television screen called "The Family"? What purpose are they supposed to serve in this society?
1.2.5 Why do Mildred and her lady friends strongly disapprove of Montag's wanting to read to them from a book? How does Mildred try to save the situation?
1.2.6 Why does Faber object to Montag's poetry reading?
1.2.7 Why do you think Mrs Phelps cried in response to Montag's reading of the poem "Dover Beach"?
1.2.8 How does Captain Beatty talk to Montag when he returns to work after his sick leave? What is unusual about it?
1.2.9 What is the effect of Beatty's manner of speaking on Montag?
1.2.10 Why is the poker game of the firemen interrupted?

1.3 Part Three of the Novel

1.3.1 How does Beatty hint at his suspicions?
1.3.2 Who must have brought the books back from the garden?
1.3.3 Who turned in an alarm against Montag?
1.3.4 How does Montag feel as he burns his own house? Why do you think he feels this way?
1.3.5 Why does Montag kill Beatty and burn his body?
1.3.6 What revelation does Montag have about Beatty after he has killed him?
1.3.7 What is Montag's plan to escape?
1.3.8 Why does Montag want Faber to turn on the air conditioning and sprinklers?
1.3.9 How is Montag's death broadcast on TV?
1.3.10 Who is Granger? What do you know about him and the group of men that are with him?

Key to Content-related Questions

1.1 Part One of the Novel

1.1.1 In the futuristic society of Bradbury's novel firemen do not extinguish fires but light them. In particular they are called to burn books as their possession is prohibited. In this role they act as guardians of the state's security.
1.1.2 As the opening indicates, "it is a pleasure to burn." Montag enjoys his job, does not question what he is doing and is a loyal fireman.
1.1.3 The way she looks, talks and behaves greatly startles Montag. Her way of walking, for example, shows that she is in harmony with nature. She notices natural elements like the dew on the grass in the morning, likes to take walks and watch the sun rise. The fact that these preferences and perceptions are singled out by her are an early indicator of her non-conforming attitude and behaviour. Apart from that she is very inquisitive and curious and asks questions that baffle the fireman Montag. Thus she wonders if Montag ever reads any of the books he burns and if it is true that once firemen put out fires instead of starting them.
1.1.4 When Montag arrives at his house he finds that the TV walls have been switched off and that the bedroom is in complete darkness. He stumbles over an empty bottle of sleeping pills and realizes that his wife Mildred has taken an overdose. He phones the emergency hospital.
1.1.5 Two fellows arrive, pump out Mildred's stomach as well as her blood and replace the latter with fresh blood and serum. The emergency treatment is done very efficiently, it is something that the operators have to do several times each night.

1.1.6 When Mildred wakes up the following morning she is hungry and feels as if she has a hangover. She does not remember anything about her suicide attempt and when confronted by Montag with her deed refuses to believe that she could have done anything like that.
1.1.7 She watches TV soaps most of the time and takes part in interactive programmes, i.e. she says missing lines that have been mailed to her. Apart from that she continually listens to music and talk shows on her ear radio. From years of listening she has learned to lip-read and does not switch the radio off when talking to her husband.
1.1.8 Clarisse is nature-minded, perceptive and thoughtful; she rarely watches the parlour walls or goes to Fun Parks. She has been made to see a psychiatrist on account of her behaviour as she does things like hiking around in forests or collecting butterflies that are obviously considered to be undesirable activities in this society.
1.1.9 The Mechanical Hound is a robotic dog that can detect the location of illegal books and is also able to kill people. It also has an olfactory system by which it can identify a person's chemical balance and, what is more, it can smell if that person is behaving in a non-conforming way. The Hound is clearly used as an instrument of terror.
1.1.10 When the Hound growls at Montag and pulls out its silver needle Montag trembles and his face turns white. He is afraid that the Hound might somehow know about the books he has hidden in the ventilator grille at his house.
1.1.11 She is considered to be "antisocial" because of her unusual behaviour. For example, she doesn't mix with people to watch TV, she prefers to talk and to ask questions in the classroom; she hasn't got any friends because her friends were killed in car racing activities; she does all her shopping and housecleaning by hand. What is more, she believes in being responsible for what she does.
1.1.12 Mildred's family are "the relatives", the various soap characters from TV whom she listens to every day, whom she "talks" to by speaking a line from a script prepared by the TV people. Her life centres exclusively around the TV parlour.
1.1.13 When Montag asks his wife for the whereabouts of Clarisse he learns that her family has moved and that she was run over and killed by a car.
1.1.14 Beatty lectures Montag on the history of the firemen, on the state's social and cultural philosophy, i.e. the need for people being made equal so as to erase differences, and the happiness principle, the absence of conflicting thoughts and opinions.

1.2 Part Two of the Novel

1.2.1 Faber is a retired Professor of English whom Montag met a few months prior to the events in the novel. He remembers him and phones him. Faber does not want to talk to him on the phone because he is afraid the fireman is setting up a trap for him.

1.2.2 Faber is critical of himself because he did not actively speak out against the development that finally led to the book-burnings, even though he was aware of it. He calls himself a coward for not having done anything against it and has become pessimistic because he thinks that now it is impossible to do anything against the burning of books. Initially Faber refuses to help Montag because of his fears, but he changes his mind when Montag starts to tear pages from the Bible he has taken along. It is then that he agrees to become Montag's teacher.

1.2.3 Before leaving Faber Montag receives a tiny radio transmitter that looks like the "Seashells" that people wear in their ears. With its help Faber and Montag will be able to keep in touch and Faber will be able to guide Montag and help him cope with difficult situations.

1.2.4 To Mildred only TV characters are real people; that is why she calls them "my family". According to her, they tell her things and they laugh when she is laughing. The family is clearly the most important thing in her life which is stressed by the fact that she is unwilling to reply to her husband's question if the family really loves her. – Programmes like "The White Clowns" tend to suppress people's individual feelings and thoughts, as they confront them with inconsequential, empty and meaningless chatter.

1.2.5 First of all, the ladies are witnesses to something illegal; secondly, they want to go on watching "The White Clowns". Mildred tries to save the situation saying that once a year a fireman is allowed to bring a book home and to read from it so that the listeners will realize how mixed-up things were in the past.

1.2.6 Faber is afraid that the reading will provoke the ladies to report Montag to the authorities. He is sure that the reading will be counterproductive and jeopardize their plans.

1.2.7 The lines that Montag reads form Matthew Arnold's poem "Dover Beach" emphasize man's sense of isolation as even love is seen as a lonely state of mind. By the end of the last verse Mrs Phelps is sobbing for no reason she can understand and Mrs Bowles begins screaming at Montag for what she considers his insensitivity.

1.2.8 Montag is reluctant to go into the firehouse, his feet are rooted to the spot in fear of Beatty. Beatty talks him into the house; he holds out his hand waiting for the book to be placed upon it by Montag, then tosses it into the fire. During the card game Beatty goes on and on quoting from various great works of literature, thereby taunting Montag and enjoying the latter's growing unease.

1.2.9 Montag becomes increasingly confused, he feels beaten and clearly cannot cope with the situation.

1.2.10 The card game is interrupted by an alarm and the firemen are called into action. We find out at the end of Part Two that Beatty has been toying with Montag all along which becomes obvious from the fact that the Captain himself drives the fire engine to its destination, which he never did before.

1.3 Part Three of the Novel

1.3.1 When standing in front of Montag's house, Beatty points out that he did give Montag hints of his suspicions by having sent the Hound around his place.

1.3.2 Montag realizes that Mildred must have watched him hide the books in the garden and brought them back inside.

1.3.3 The first alarm was turned in by Mildred's lady friends, but the Captain "let it ride" (p. 152). The second alarm was put in by Mildred herself. When Mildred is leaving the house and climbing into a taxi she does not even once acknowledge her husband's presence.

1.3.4 Beatty is not content to simply torch the house, he wants Montag to do it, by using a blowtorch. Montag does as he is told. As he starts to torch one room and then the next he begins to take great pleasure in destroying his home. His pleasure stems from the realization that by burning down his house he will change his former life, will literally cleanse it.

1.3.5 After Beatty has knocked the transmitter bullet out of Montag's ear and threatens to have his friend arrested, Montag twitches the safety catch on the flame-thrower. Beatty's constant taunting and the fear for his only friend's life drive him to the desperate act of killing the Captain.

1.3.6 Later on Montag realizes that Beatty wanted to die. He not only continued to taunt Montag knowing how desperate he was, but did not really do anything to prevent his own death.

1.3.7 As Montag gets away from the scene of his crime he puts his seashell radio into his ear to find out if he can get any information about being chased by the authorities. The announcer is telling the listeners to watchout for a man on the run. Hearing the report Montag immediately stops running and strolls to a petrol station where he cleans himself in the bathroom. Then he begins to walk calmly towards Faber's flat.

1.3.8 He instructs Faber to do this so that the Mechanical Hound cannot pick up any scent.

1.3.9 After Montag has crossed the river and reached the book people he watches his fake death on a portable TV. An innocent person is used as an ersatz victim, a camera films the Hound's seizing that person. As the person's face is never shown in any close-up no one can doubt the announcer's claim that Montag has been killed.

1.3.10 Granger is the leader of a small group of people. He is the first to speak to Montag, introduces his collegues and explains their duty as living books. He offers Montag to join them. He informs him about their network and after the atomic bombing draws the analogy between the mythical bird Phoenix and the history of mankind thereby instilling hope in the others.

2. Interpreting Different Aspects of the Novel

2.1 Compare and evaluate the characterizations of Clarisse and Mildred. What do you make of the fact that Clarisse is introduced first?
2.2 Analyze the relationship between Montag and Mildred.
2.3 Describe Montag's development from a committed fireman to a dissident. Discuss the causes for his change of attitude.
2.4 In various contexts mention is made of Montag's hands. Examine these contexts and show how the use of hands corresponds to Montag's mental changes.
2.5 Characterize Mildred's way of life.
2.6 Work out the major ideas Beatty presents in his lecture to Montag. Consider the rhetorical devices he uses and analyze their respective roles in this situation.
2.7 Describe Faber's role in the novel and characterize him.
2.8 Analyze the relationships between the central characters with regard to the protagonist.
2.9 At the beginning of the novel the nozzle Montag is holding in his hands is compared to a python. Other animal imagery refers to the medical equipment of the technicians who pump out Mildred's stomach and to the mythical bird Phoenix. Analyze this imagery.
2.10 Work out the various science fiction elements Bradbury uses in this novel.
2.11 While Montag is swimming across the river he has many reveries. What does he dream about? What is the effect of these reveries on his state of mind?
2.12 Describe the book people in the forest. What is their way of life like, what are their intentions?
2.13 Discuss the role of the book people as opponents to the mainstream society. In what way do they present a viable alternative? How convincing do you find this dissident group?
2.14 Describe the dystopian structure of the novel and determine the function of its parts.

Key to Interpreting Different Aspects of the Novel

2.1 From the very beginning the seventeen-year-old Clarisse is introduced as an imaginative, kind, intuitive, creative and intelligent person that is interested in the world around her. She does not watch the TV walls nor does she go to the amusement parks like her classmates. She dislikes going to school as school seems intent to make her an exact duplicate of her classmates and she will not agree to give up her individuality. She has no friends or relationships with her peers.

The teenage girl is a new neighbour of Montag's. She questions the rationale that governs his life as a fireman and becomes the stimulus that makes Montag begin to doubt what he is doing. Significantly, the colour white is associated with her, underlining her innocence and her moral purity.
She is an observing person, a lover of nature, and notices smells and natural things like the morning dew. Unlike most people in this society she is communicative and remembers the past. Her family later disappears in the novel and she is said to have been killed by a car.
The contrast between Mildred, Montag and Clarisse McClellan becomes immediately obvious. Mildred is in a state of living death as symbolically expressed by the mausoleum-like darkness that surrounds her. When Montag comes home and opens their bedroom door he enters a tomb-world in which his wife's sleeping body is compared to a body that is displayed on the lid of a tomb. The fact that Clarisse is introduced first indicates that she will play an important role in Montag's life.

2.2 The couple's relationship is marked by a lack of communication and understanding. Mildred has no desire to converse with her husband or in any way interact with him, unless it is to ask him to provide her with a fourth TV wall. Montag cannot comprehend her obsession with the faces on the screen and their meaningless babble. He continually tries to understand her interest and even attempts to use it as a means to communicate with his wife, but since there is no substance to this form of entertainment there is nothing to talk about. When he is upset about her attempted suicide and tries to discuss what happened and why, Mildred remains numb and mindless; she is unwilling, perhaps unable, to acknowledge her apparent deep unhappiness.
The lack of mutual understanding and the couple's estrangement come into focus when comparing their different reactions to the burning of the old woman. While the recollection of the circumstances makes Montag vomit, Mildred's only concern is the rag that has become dirty. The incident shows that Mildred is insensitive and uncaring, that she has no concern for her husband.
Their relationship is only viable as long as Montag is content with his job as a fireman. When he begins to question what he is doing, when he starts wondering about his wife's mindless TV consumption, Mildred becomes upset. She is particularly irritated when he brings some books with him and wants them to read from the books together. When Montag recites poetry in front of her friends she reports on him, thus ending their relationship. All in all it can be said that their marriage is not founded on mutual trust and understanding. It is apparent that they cannot exchange ideas freely and that there is no sense of togetherness in their lives.

2.3 Guy Montag as the novel's protagonist is the central character. *Fahrenheit 451* deals with his transformation from an obedient servant of the state to a questioning individual. He takes pride in his work, his job is like an art to him that he carries out with great joy as the opening scene of the novel indicates. He becomes curious, however, after meeting and talking to his young neighbour Clarisse who confronts him during their first encounter with his mental and emotional apathy. On account of their second encounter Montag begins having doubts about his job as a fireman and begins to realize that his is a loveless life.

When he meets Clarisse for the third time she confronts him with the meaninglessness of his life, thus setting in motion a process of re-evaluation. The change in Montag is noticed by the Mechanical Hound who starts to threaten him. Montag begins to feel guilty, but is not yet able at this stage to recognize what has triggered off this feeling. After the incident with the old woman he instinctively takes a book with him, breaking the rules of the firemen and thus showing a first sign of disobedience. His internal conflict grows and he reacts physically as well as psychologically. He develops a fever and has to vomit and becomes disgusted with himself. Captain Beatty's lecture leaves no impression on him other than to re-enforce his desire to read the books he has hidden in his house. Through his contact with a former Professor of English, Faber, Montag is further exposed to the content of books. Moreover, Faber's lecture on the need for leisure as opposed to mere entertainment and on the need for individual self-determination opens his eyes and makes him becoming a dissident. His reading poetry to his wife's friends is a clear violation of society's laws and shows that he has started to challenge the system they live in and rebel against it. Montag's transformation becomes fully apparent when he is burning his own house. He not only puts an end to the relationship with Mildred and eradicates the life he has lived so far, but, what is more, he destroys his position in the system and eradicates his old self as a fireman. For the first time, burning has become a positive act for him. When swimming in the river he discovers his desire for something permanent in his life, he recognizes that he has a responsibility to preserve mankind and its cultural heritage. His joining the book people completes this process of transformation.

2.4 When Montag is introduced to the reader in the opening description his hands are compared to the hands of a conductor directing an orchestra. Later when he steals a book from the library of the old woman that is about to be burnt this act is described as having been carried out by autonomous hands with a brain of their own. Similarly, when Faber initially refuses to help him, Montag's hands, by themselves, begin to rip pages from the books he has brought along. And when sitting at a table with his superior Captain Beatty Montag's fingers are compared to ferrets that have done some evil and he feels the guilt of his hands. When reflecting on his killing Beatty Montag cannot decide whether his hands or Beatty's reaction to the hands gave him "the final push toward murder". Throughout the novel Montag's hands mediate his inner conflicts and illustrate his inner change.

2.5 Mildred's way of life is marked, first of all, by her excessive consumerism. Her only pleasure in life is her television walls and the soap people who talk about nothing meaningful or important. She shows no interest in her environment or even in other people. When she feels upset she jumps in her car and drives very fast in order to forget whatever has upset her. Acting impulsively and not thinking about the consequences is one major characteristic of her way of life. Another refers to her continuous dependence on some form of external distraction. When she is not watching the walls, she has the little "Seashells" in her ears that play music or report news. Thus she has completely isolated herself from her surroundings. Her way of life mirrors the main beliefs of the society she lives in: she is completely conformist, devoid of any critical thought, superficial and shallow.

2.6 Beatty outlines in his lecture to Montag the ideology of the dystopian society. Their respective roles are clear from the beginning: Beatty is the benevolent representative of the system who is talking to his disciple Montag, explaining to him how the system works, how it came about and what roles the firemen play in it. Hence his lecture is highly didactic.

He begins his lecture with a history of the firemen and the reasons for their coming into existence, then goes on to talk about the hedonistic principle underlying life in this society, refers to the need for conformity and alikeness and finally stresses the task of the firemen to ensure the happiness of the people. His lecture is mainly made up of assertions and examples. According to him, books are a source of unhappiness; as they are subversive they must be destroyed in order to keep the people from being confronted with conflicting and confusing thoughts. Hence books were first made simple, their complexity was literally erased, then they were reduced to comics and finally forbidden. Superior minds and non-conformist intellectuals are said to cause trouble and unrest, therefore they must be made to conform to the rest, if necessary, by enforced psychiatric means. The sole aim of life as Beatty sees it is the pursuit of pleasure; happiness is not a state of mind but an activity which is a duty. Society is based by and large on conformity, egalitarianism and excessive consumerism; people live in the present, there is no past nor any future, as there exist no visions in this society. Throughout his lecture Beatty never seeks to prove his assertions and statements. He does not present any arguments; instead, he uses strings of enumeration which he literally hammers into Montag. His rhetoric thus reflects his superior status, there is no need for him to justify anything, it is sufficient to praise the achievements of this society.

2.7 Faber is in many ways the intellectual antagonist of Beatty. He criticizes the system, pointing out its deficits and explains these to Montag. Hence he becomes Montag's intellectual mentor. Initially he is portrayed as a coward, as a fellow traveller who saw the negative development of society but was unable or unwilling to speak out against it. When Montag tears out pages from what is probably the only copy of the Bible left, thereby deeply shocking the book-lover Faber, he lets himself be provoked into becoming an accomplice and active supporter. Even though he does not turn into an activist, he helps Montag to escape to the book people.

2.8 All the characters are more or less defined in their relation to the protagonist Montag, and may be grouped accordingly. In accordance with the bi-partite structure of the dystopian world the tableau of characters is also arranged in a bi-partite way. There are the representatives of the mainstream society like Mildred and her friends who encorporate the basic beliefs of this society. Naturally, Beatty as the main spokesman also falls into this category. These representatives are contrasted by those characters who represent the otherworld: Clarisse, Faber and Granger. Within the overall structure Clarisse and Faber serve as contrasts to Mildred and Beatty.
With regard to the characters' roles, the following has to be stated: Beatty is the spokesman of the system, Faber the critic and hence his functional antagonist. The same role may be ascribed to Granger, who also explains the dissident otherworld to Montag. Clarisse, on the other hand, serves as a catalyst for Montag's transformation from subservient fireman to rebel.

2.9 The image of the snake is used to describe the firemen's hoses and the machine that sucks out Mildred's poisoned blood. In the first instance the python represents the destructive use of fire, in the second case it stands for the inability of the paramedics to do away all the poison that Mildred has symbolically accumulated over the years. The cobra-like machine cannot really cure Mildred as it does not affect her state of mind. Hence her state of mind that has been poisoned by her mindless TV watching cannot be neutralized by applying technical devices. – The image of the Phoenix used by Granger towards the end of the novel (cf. pp. 208 f) is a sign of hope. When describing the bird and its habit of burning himself up and getting himself reborn, Granger draws an analogy between the mythical bird and men, expressing his hope that mankind will also be reborn after the atomic destruction of the city.

2.10 The book depicts an unknown future country, possibly the United States, where a form of interactive television dominates culture and all books are banned. As a fireman Montag is the member of an elite, repressive group whose purpose it is to seek out and burn the few books that have remained. The rules of society demand total conformity; intellectual curiosity and independent thought have been replaced by apathy and passivity. Mildred and her friends, for example, never even wonder about their cause in life, they are content with whatever entertainment they receive from TV and have no intellectual grasp of what the coming war might mean to them. Seen in this light, the novel addresses the issues of mass-media-induced illiteracy and anti-intellectualism that Bradbury foresaw at the beginning of the 1950s.

The book-burnings as well as the various references to political repression and conformity are reminiscent of historical events that the author has projected into the future, e.g. the book-burnings by the Nazis or the censorship-inspired campaign against un-American activities by Senator Joseph McCarthy in the 1950s that has led to a total censorship of all reading material.

The single element typical of science fiction is undoubtedly the creation of the Mechanical Hound. Bradbury presents a robot that is more powerful than a human being in its ability to locate its prey. This reflects the commonly held view in the 1950s that robots are to be feared because they might be able to take control over human beings. Bradbury satirizes this fear by portraying a monstrous creature that is used as an instrument of terror and repression.

2.11 After Montag has escaped the Hound and is swimming in the river he is literally embraced by its peaceful silence. Floating in the water is like a spiritual cleansing for him. Being carried along by the flow of the water symbolizes a new starting-point in life. Montag is given the time to ponder the events which have brought him to this point. He thinks of his wife and wonders if the silence would drive her mad. He then fantasizes about sleeping in a barn from the window of which he can see a beautiful young woman doing her hair as she sits in a window of her farmhouse. In the morning he would find a cool glass of milk, an apple and a pear waiting for him at the foot of the barn steps. The young girl is, of course, reminiscent of Clarisse who gave him the comfort of food and drink for his soul. When Montag leaves the embrace of the water and the comfort of his reverie, he is confronted with the smells and sounds of the forest. The reveries have prepared him for these new perceptions.

2.12 When Montag has reached the other side of the river and enters the forest he is overwhelmed by the abundance of nature. He feels no longer afraid, the forest is like a shelter for him. The book people he meets there are society's outcasts, former scholars who have become living books by having memorized literary texts. They are nomads who have survived because they do not have books in their possession and are thus left alone by the authorities. They live a simple, rural life without the luxuries and technological goods that the mainstream society provides. The sole aim of their life is to store mankind's cultural treasures and to pass them on to future generations.

2.13 On the one hand, it could be argued that the book people do not constitute a plausible opposition to the totalitarian mainstream society as their vision seems to be rather naive. Even when their leader Granger speaks of a network of thousands of like-minded people, the reader is left wondering how these people will ever be able to achieve what they want to achieve. One is also left wondering what kind of future the book people will have as survivors of the atomic attack. Moreover, the optimism voiced by Granger in his example of the phoenix seems construed and artificial, there is nothing in the novel's plot that would prepare mankind for such a surprise ending. On the other hand, it has to be pointed out that *Fahrenheit 451* is a novel of ideas in which Bradbury stresses the need for intellectual freedom and seeks to defend literacy and the use of imagination as central human virtues. If viewed in this light, the characters and their actions are embodiments of these ideas rather than full-fledged characters with a life of their own.

2.14 In *Fahrenheit 451* Bradbury juxtaposes a totalitarian dystopian world with an idyllic otherworld which is in many ways a reversal of the mainstream world. The mainstream world is an extrapolation of certain contemporary features (e.g. excessive TV consumerism) and of recent historical events (e.g. the book-burnings in Nazi Germany). The idyllic otherworld, by contrast, is retrospective in character, as it is conservative and reminiscent of a peaceful life in harmony with nature. Within the novel the otherworld functions as a mirror to accentuate the defects and shortcomings of the mainstream world.

3. Truffaut's Film

3.1 Work out the major differences between the film and the novel and evaluate them.

3.2 Analyze Julie Christie's double role as Linda (Mildred) and Clarisse. Consider in this context Christie's own view as presented in the DVD's bonus material.

3.3 Examine the credits at the beginning and at the end of the film. What are their effects?

3.4 Interpret the filming of the fire engine when being driven to its scene of action. Consider the camera shots, movements and the choice of music.

3.5 Analyze in detail the scene in which Montag reads from a book for the first time.

3.6 Write your own film review.

Key to Truffaut's Film

3.1 The central ideas presented by the novel, i.e. the role of firemen, the function of Clarisse, Mildred's shallow and empty life, her TV addiction and Montag's transformation from obedient servant to rebel have all been taken up in the film. And just as in the novel there is the otherworld with its book people. Differences refer to omissions and to changes in the tableau of figures. There is no Mechanical Hound and Faber has been left out. The characters of Mildred (Linda) and Clarisse are played by the same actress. Furthermore, there is no atomic war at the end of the film and unlike in the novel Clarisse stays alive. Montag meets her again, when Granger is showing him around the site of the book people and introducing him to a large number of living books. The enumeration of the titles illustrates that mankind's heritage is being preserved here (ironically, Truffaut has also one character embody Ray Bradbury's *The Martian Chronicles*).
Granger does not use the parable of the Phoenix to voice his optimism; in a sermon-like tone he delivers the following speech:

> "Oh, it wasn't planned. It just so happened that a man here and a man there loved some book. And rather than lose it, he learned it. And we came together. We're a minority of undesirables crying out in the wilderness. But it won't always be so. One day, we shall be called on, one by one, to recite what we have learned. And then books will be printed again. And when the next age of darkness comes, those who come after us will do as we have done." *(Verbatim transcript from the film)*

Hence the film's ending is even more ambiguous and vague than that of the novel. Despite the obvious differences it should be noted that the script of the film largely follows the plot presented in the novel. The omission of

Faber may be defended on the ground that Clarisse's role as instigator of Montag's change is sufficiently apparent. And having left out the Mechanical Hound was probably a wise decision considering the technical possibilities of trick filming in the mid-1960s. Instead, the film focusses on the presentation of Montag's wife, her character and way of life, and on the burning of the library of the old woman.

3.2 In the *Feature Commentary with Julie Christie* which is part of the bonus material of the DVD the actress calls the doubling of roles a "cinematic device for showing different sides of human beings." She then goes on to note that these sides refer to the question whether a person makes a conscious choice, e.g. whether he or she is brainwashed or not. What Julie Christie seems to stress here is the co-existence of obedience and resistance inside a person with regard to his or her dealing with a totalitarian society. Which of the two sides prevail in a given situation is a question of choice. Additionally it is to be pointed out that the dialogue between Montag and Clarisse during their first meeting gives a hint at the double role of the female protagonist. Asked by Clarisse what his wife is like, he answers: "She's rather like you. Quite like you." Montag's answer reveals his unconscious wish to have his wife be like Clarisse.

3.3 The spoken credits at the beginning foreshadow the fact that the society depicted in the film has forbidden the reading and writing of books. Each name that is spoken corresponds to one shot in the montage; the sequence of shots is rapid, with each shot there is a zoom-in on TV antennas. As each shot is tinted in a different colour, an impression of discontinuity is created here. Surprisingly, in the film's ending there are no credits either, as it ends with a long, slow zoom-out shot of the books people's camp in the woods where they are seen walking around a lake reciting their books. Their voices mingle together and grow fainter as a slow, homophonic music is to be heard. The shot with which the film ends thus refers us back to its beginning. While most films usually end with the credits which mark a sharp caesura and therefore allow the audience to dissociate themselves from what they have seen, there is no such definite end to *Fahrenheit 451*. Rather, the final scene of this film is closely connected with its beginning thus inviting the audience to review what they have seen and to think about it.

3.4 The fire engine is shown four times when being driven to its scene of action (cf. chapters 1, 4, 10 and 14 of the DVD). Each time the camera tracks the movement of the engine by long shots, thereby creating the impression that the engine dominates the space which it is crossing. There is nothing that might stop it on its way, it seems to be too powerful. This impression is re-enforced by the use of the colour red and the staccato-like music with its insistent rhythm that accompanies the driving engine. The engine is almost personified here, its menacing nature endows it with qualities associated with the police in totalitarian terror regimes.

3.5 When Montag returns home from work he goes into the bathroom to hide some books. When he is about to leave the room, he turns off the light. The darkness is captured on the screen for several seconds, thus emphasizing the outrageous nature of what he has done. There is a cut and then Montag is shown getting up from his bed and fetching a book. He switches on the light of the TV wall and sits with his back next to the blank wall. He is filmed from a slight low angle, holding a book in his hands and starting to read. There is a view over his shoulder as he begins to read out the title, the author's name and the publisher. Then the camera zooms in on the page, then on a paragraph, after that on a line and focusses on just one word as it follows Montag's finger along the line. The camera pans to follow the text at the rate of Montag's slow reading. The scene underlines several aspects: it stresses Montag's isolation, as he is compelled to read secretly, and reveals that he has difficulties both in reading and in grasping the meaning of what he is reading. Next it establishes a symbolic contrast between his reading and the TV parlour. Sitting with his back to the wall Montag symbolically rejects TV in favour of reading.

3.6 A film review should provide essential information about the film which will help to decide whether or not to go and see that film. Hence any review should include the following points:

- *Credits:* these include the title of the film and the year in which it was released, its genre, director and the names of the main actors.
- *Plot:* here a brief summary should be presented, however the ending should not be mentioned; information about where and when the action takes place is necessary and mention should be made of the presentation of time in the film. Is it chronological or are there flashbacks? Furthermore, background information on the setting and the social classes should be given.
- *Characters:* here you refer to the physical and psychological peculiarities of the characters, their relationships, their age and their political or cultural background.
- *Performance:* briefly deal with one or two actors and their performance; give examples from the film and back your assessment by arguments.
- *Conclusion:* describe your reaction to the film and give a final evaluation.

For model reviews you may check the digital editions of any of the major British quality papers or www.rottentomatoes.com

4. Creative Writing

4.1 Imagine the story were to be continued, how would you let it go on?

4.2 Write an alternative ending to the given ending of the novel leaving out the atomic bombing of the city.

4.3 Write a letter to the editor of the *New York Times*. Discuss the review by Bosley Crowther (see pp. 57 f in this study aid). Regardless of whether you agree or disagree with his critical points, be sure to use arguments of your own either to support what he said or to refute it.

4.4 More than half a century has passed since *Fahrenheit 451* was published and more than 40 years have gone by since the film by French director François Truffaut came into the cinemas. Write a letter to a Hollywood producer trying to convince him of a remake.

Key to Creative Writing

4.1 The novel has an open ending, hence it makes a provoking appeal to the reader to speculate on alternative endings.
- What do you expect to happen?
- Will Montag meet his wife Mildred again? Will Mildred have changed on account of the atomic war?
- Will Faber make it to St. Louis and persuade the old printer whom he knows there to reprint books?
- Will the bookmen persuade the survivors of the atomic blast to change their way of life?
- Will there be an uprising within the mainstream society by the survivors who feel deceived by their government?

4.2 Here you might wish to describe how an alternative movement develops as the book people get together and start a march of protest.

4.3 You could use the following arguments in your letter-to-the-editor:
- Crowther has written a slating rather than a well-reasoned review.
- Individual points of criticism are value judgements that are hardly ever backed up by examples from the film or by arguments.
- The writer's attitude towards the French director is condescending and thereby biased.
- The structure of the review shows the writer's dislike for the film: he opens his text with a verdict and closes it with a negative pun.

4.4 Here you have to argue carefully as you want to convince the producer. You may want to make use of the following suggestions:
- Point out the negative reception of the film by the *New York Times*, mention the critic's negative view of Oskar Werner's performance ("dismal, unexciting") and quote the critic's calling the film "bloodless and pom-

pous". You should be able either to support or to refute this verdict by giving at least one example from the film.

- Refer to Bradbury's own criticism (in "The Making of *Fahrenheit 451*", DVD, Bonus Material) where he deplores the absence of the Mechanical Hound and calls it "a flaw".
- List your suggestions as to which aspects of the novel's plot you wish to concentrate on and state your reasons.

  If you wish to make suggestions for the casting, do so, but explain why you want to have a particular actor or actress for a specific role.

Bibliography

Bradbury, Ray, *A Medicine For Melancholy*, New York: Bantam, 1971. ["The Smile", pp. 110–115.]

– *The Illustrated Man*, New York: Bantam, 1972. ["The Exiles", pp. 94–105.]

– *The Martian Chronicles*, New York: Bantam, 1975. ["Usher II", pp. 103–118.]

– "Burning Bright" (Afterword), in: R. B., *Fahrenheit 451*, London: Harper-Voyager, 2008, pp. 215–227.

– *Fahrenheit 451*, directed by François Truffaut (1966), DVD, Universal Pictures Germany GmbH, 2003.

– "The Making of *Fahrenheit 451*", DVD, Bonus Material.

Bloom, Herold, ed., *Modern Critical Interpretations: Ray Bradbury's "Fahrenheit 451"*, Philadelphia: Chelsea House Publishers, 2003.

Christopher, John, *The Guardians*, London: Puffin, 1973.

Eller, Jonathan R. / Touponce, William F., *Ray Bradbury: The Life of Fiction*, Kent/London: The Kent State University Press, 2004.

Geirland, John, "Bradbury's Tomorrowland", www.wired.com/1998/10/bradbury

Huxley, Aldous, *Brave New World*, London: Flamingo Modern Classic, 1994.

Miller, John J., "The Man Who Sounded The Fire Alarm – 'Fahrenheit 451', 50 Years Later", in: *The Wall Street Journal*, May 14, 2003, https://www.wjs.com/articles/SB105288055761123900

Nolan, William F. / Greenberg, Martin H., eds., *Science Fiction Origins*, New York: Fawcett, 1980. ["The Fireman", pp. 9–70; "Editor's Afterword", pp. 71 f.]

Postman, Neil, *Amusing Ourselves to Death. Public Discourse in the Age of Show Business,* New York: Viking, 1985.

Przybyszewski, Chris, "*Fahrenheit 451:* 50th Anniversay Edition", in: *SF Site: Feature Reviews,* 2005, www.sfsite.com/01b/fh192/htm

Real, Willi, "The Use of Literary Quotations and Allusions in Ray Bradbury, *Fahrenheit 451*", www.heliweb.de/telic/bradcom.htm

Smith, Jeremy, "The Failure of *Fahrenheit 451*", in: *Strange Horizons,* October 13, 2003, www.strangehorizons.com/non-fiction/articles/the-failure-of-fahrenheit-451